JULIAN HAWTHORNE

Incredible Mysteries: Unsolved Disappearances Vol. 1

Contents

Introduction

I n the heart of our civilized world, amidst the rhythm of daily life and the forward march of progress, there exists an unsettling and often overlooked reality – the phenomenon of missing persons. These are not mere statistics; they are poignant stories of individuals who vanished into thin air, leaving behind a trail of questions, a whirlwind of emotions, and an enduring enigma. Explore some of the most perplexing and haunting unsolved missing persons cases across the globe.

These narratives, steeped in mystery, defy explanation and ignite the imagination. Each case is a labyrinth, a complex interplay of clues, theories, and conjectures. Spanning from quiet suburban neighborhoods to remote wilderness, bustling urban centers to serene rural areas, these disappearances cut across the fabric of society and geography, underscoring that the mystery of the missing knows no boundaries.

The true stories here are compelling and heart-wrenching. They involve everyday people whose lives were abruptly interrupted – individuals who left for routine activities and mysteriously vanished. Their disappearances have puzzled investigators, confounded experts, and left families and communities in a state of perpetual uncertainty, holding onto hope against seemingly insurmountable odds.

Dive deeply into the emotional and psychological impact of these cases. It's not only about the missing but also about those left behind. Families, friends, and communities grapple with the gaping void left by these unexplained disappearances. Their journeys through grief, frustration, and relentless hope are critical to comprehending the full scope of these mysteries. Their voices and their resilience form a poignant testament to human endurance.

Examine the investigative challenges these cases present. Explore the difficulties faced by law enforcement, the evolution of search and rescue operations, and the advancements in forensic science that kindle new hope in solving these mysteries. The narrative scrutinizes the role of media in shaping public perception and addresses the often-overlooked phenomenon of missing persons who do not fit the conventional profile that attracts widespread attention.

Confronting the darker and more elusive aspects of human experience, the narrative grapples with the unknown and faces the unsettling truth that some mysteries, despite our best efforts, remain unsolved. Yet, even in the absence of closure, these stories impart valuable lessons about resilience, the human spirit, and the enduring quest for answers.

As you delve into this exploration, approach with an open mind and a compassionate heart. Remember, each case represents real people and real lives touched by mystery. Welcome to a world of shadows and echoes, where the search for the missing continues, and the quest for answers is an ever-evolving journey.

Sky Metalwala

The saga of Sky Metalwala's parents, both immigrants to the United States, unfolds with a blend of cultural backgrounds and personal struggles. Solomon Metalwala, hailing from Pakistan, had established his life in Bellevue, Washington, where he managed a convenience store. It was in this setting in 1997 that he met Julia Biryukova, a Ukrainian native who had a turbulent childhood in Soviet Russia. Julia's past was marked by harrowing experiences in mental hospitals where she was subjected to shock therapy as punishment and endured severe disciplinary beatings from her parents, leaving deep scars on her self-esteem.

Julia's journey to the United States began at the age of 12 when she emigrated from Russia. By the time she was 15, as a student at Bellevue High School, her path crossed with Solomon, then 21. A chance invitation to a party led to the start of their relationship. Julia soon became involved in Solomon's life, taking up a job at a restaurant owned by his family in Seattle's Pioneer Square. Their lives became increasingly intertwined, and by 1999, following Julia's high school graduation and her naturalization, they made a significant commitment by purchasing a condominium together in Bellevue.

However, the relationship between Biryukova and Metalwala was not without its challenges. Despite sharing work and leisure activities, tensions surfaced, notably during a loud argument at a Kirkland gas station, drawing police attention. During this incident, a man identifying himself as Sulaiman Metalwala, believed to be Solomon's brother, was involved.

As the relationship progressed, Biryukova confided in a clinical psychologist about the controlling nature of her boyfriend, revealing her growing emotional dependency on him. This complex dynamic led to their marriage in 2003, conducted hastily in Solomon's mother's kitchen. According to Biryukova, she was coerced into the marriage under the threat of Solomon's alleged impending deportation and the ultimatum of never seeing him again if she refused. The true reasons behind this rushed union remained a secret from her family until 2010.

In 2005, a significant shift occurred when Solomon embraced Christianity, leading the couple to join a church in Kirkland. This decision, however, seemed to have unintended consequences on Julia's relationship with her in-laws, who she felt blamed her for this religious transition, further complicating their already strained marital dynamics.

The next few years were marked by mounting challenges. Financial strains began to emerge around 2007 when a rival deli opened next to their restaurant, significantly impacting their earnings. It was during this turbulent time that they welcomed their first child, Maile, bringing a glimmer of joy amidst their growing concerns.

The onset of the Great Recession in 2008 added to their difficulties, yet, undeterred by their financial predicament, the couple ambitiously purchased a home in Kirkland for over $800,000. This was in addition to the mortgage they were already servicing on their Bellevue condominium, reflecting a blend of optimism and financial imprudence.

2009 brought another major life event with the birth of their son, Sky. During her pregnancy, Julia was prescribed antidepressants by a psychiatrist, a decision she disagreed with, indicating an undercurrent of psychological stress. This period also saw the beginning of their financial collapse, as lenders started foreclosing on their properties due to mounting arrears. The family was forced to downsize, moving from their Kirkland home back to their smaller Bellevue residence.

Amidst these financial and housing upheavals, the couple's relationship further deteriorated. Solomon, in later court documents, claimed that Julia developed obsessive behaviors, compelling him to adapt his living habits drastically, including eating outside and sleeping on the floor to conform to her stringent cleanliness standards for the condominium. Their lifestyle became a source of disturbance in their community, leading to several complaints for noise violations, including instances of late-night vacuuming.

The most alarming incident, however, occurred when Sky was just two months old. The parents faced a serious legal situation after leaving Sky alone in their car in a Target parking lot for nearly an hour on a bitterly cold day, with temperatures plummeting to 27 °F. Although they claimed to have been away for only twenty minutes, not wanting to disturb their sleeping child, security footage from the store contradicted their account. They were arrested and charged with reckless endangerment. This incident cast a stark light on the couple's parenting, leading to significant scrutiny. The charges were eventually dropped years later after the couple agreed to undergo a parenting class.

The tumultuous relationship between Julia Biryukova and Solomon Metalwala reached a critical juncture around Julia's 29th birthday in early 2010. In a distressing turn of events, Julia was committed to a mental hospital for the first time after revealing to Solomon that she had experienced a troubling dream about harming their children. During her hospitalization, she was diagnosed with severe obsessive-compulsive disorder (OCD). Despite this diagnosis, the psychiatrists did not consider her unfit for parenting, a claim Julia would later deny, adding layers of complexity to her mental health narrative.

In the wake of her release from the hospital, Solomon initiated divorce proceedings, marking the beginning of a new and turbulent chapter in their lives. During their separation, Julia sent texts to Solomon expressing suicidal thoughts, which she later admitted were attempts to capture his attention. Her mental health continued to be a significant concern, as evidenced by her Global Assessment of Functioning score during her third hospitalization, indicating a severe impairment initially, which improved only marginally upon her release.

Following this release, Solomon and his brother took a proactive step by accompanying Julia to the University of Washington Medical Center, where she checked in voluntarily. Around the same time, they faced another setback as their lender foreclosed on their condominium. Solomon, adapting to these changing circumstances, moved with the children to his parents' home in Kirkland.

The divorce proceedings that ensued were fraught with accusations and counter-accusations. Julia alleged that Solomon was abusive and expressed fear for her life, while Solomon contended that these claims were fabricated and pointed to Julia's mental health issues and obsessive behaviors as reasons for her inability to provide adequately for the children, including maintaining a proper home environment. Child Protective Services investigated an allegation against Solomon for injuring his daughter but found it to be baseless. Despite this, he faced a year-long separation from his children during the investigation. Throughout the legal battle, both spouses sought protective orders against each other, illustrating the depth of their animosity and distrust.

In a significant legal decision in September 2010, the court granted Julia full custody of the children. She exercised this control by denying Solomon any visitation rights, further fueling the conflict. Solomon remained persistent in court, addressing not only the custody issue but also matters related to shared property. Julia proposed moving to Arizona with the children in exchange for waiving alimony and child support, but Solomon rejected this offer, leading to continued legal entanglements.

This contentious period extended for over a year. In November 2011, the court mandated a week of mediation for the couple, aiming to resolve their disputes. The session appeared to be a breakthrough, with the couple agreeing to grant Julia custody and Solomon full visitation rights. However, this accord was short-lived. Julia, feeling pressured during the mediation, called her lawyer to void the agreement.

On a fateful morning in November 2011, an event unfolded that would captivate public attention and add a mysterious chapter to the already complex narrative of Julia Biryukova and her family. Julia recounted that on November 6, her son Sky, unwell at the time, needed medical attention. Determined to get him the care he needed, she bundled up Sky and his sister Maile into her 1998 silver Acura Integra and set off towards Overlake Medical Center in Bellevue.

Julia's journey, however, took an unexpected turn. As she drove along the 2600 block of 112th Avenue N.E. in Bellevue, a road skirting a tall concrete noise barrier near the curve of the Washington State Route 520 expressway, just west of its junction with Interstate 405, her car suddenly ran out of gas. This unforeseen situation forced Julia to make a quick decision.

With her car stranded by the roadside, Julia made the choice to leave Sky, still strapped in his car seat, as she and Maile ventured out in search of help. Their quest for assistance led them to a Chevron gas station about a mile north from where the car was parked. This journey took them roughly an hour.

Once at the gas station, instead of purchasing gas or seeking help to bring it back to her car, Julia contacted a friend. This friend promptly arrived, providing Julia and Maile a ride back to the car. However, upon their return, Julia was met with a shocking and distressing discovery: Sky was no longer in the car. In a state of panic, she immediately notified the police to report her son missing.

The police, in response to Julia's alarming report, swiftly contacted Solomon before noon that same day. This sequence of events set in motion a series of investigations and speculations, deeply entangling the already troubled lives of Julia and Solomon and plunging them into a new realm of public scrutiny and personal anguish.

In the aftermath of Julia Biryukova's alarming report, search teams scoured a 20-block radius around the car where Sky was last seen, yet their efforts yielded no trace of the missing child. As the Bellevue police delved deeper into the case, they began to harbor doubts about the credibility of Biryukova's account.

Upon examination, Biryukova's car, which she claimed had run out of gas, was found to have a sufficient fuel supply and functioned without issue. This crucial discovery contradicted her initial statement and cast a shadow of suspicion over her narrative. Furthermore, during the hour Biryukova reportedly spent searching for help before reaching the gas station, there was little evidence to suggest she made significant efforts to seek assistance from nearby residents. Adding to the puzzling scenario, Biryukova had left her home with her allegedly sick child without her wallet, purse, or phone, essentials for any emergency situation. Notably, no gas can was found in her car, deepening the mystery.

When confronted with these inconsistencies, Biryukova chose to invoke her Fifth Amendment rights, refusing to participate in a lie detector test. However, she did allow investigators to search her car, computer, and home. The searches turned up no signs of Sky at any of these locations. Her car was found unlocked, with no evidence of forced entry. The police also searched Solomon Metalwala's house but found nothing of relevance. Solomon himself underwent a lie detector test the night after Sky's disappearance, which was inconclusive, followed by another test the next day. The results of these tests were not made public by either him, his attorney, or the police.

The police investigation uncovered the 2009 incident where Biryukova and

Solomon were arrested for leaving Sky unattended in their car. During the investigation, both parents admitted to having occasionally left the children alone for extended periods. Detectives did not confirm rumors that Biryukova might have left the children alone during the lengthy mediation hearing the week before Sky's disappearance.

A puzzling aspect of the case was whether Sky had actually been in the car on the morning he disappeared. Motorists who had passed the parked Acura reported nothing unusual, including the absence of a child in the vehicle. Neighbors at Biryukova's apartment complex in Redmond noted that she and her children were seldom seen outdoors, and none had seen Sky for at least two weeks prior to his disappearance. Solomon was also unaware of anyone other than his ex-wife who had seen his son since a doctor's visit in April. However, Sky's sister Maile told the police that Sky had indeed been in the car that morning.

The case took a more intriguing turn when the police discovered a striking similarity between Biryukova's story and a plot from a recent episode of the NBC crime drama "Law & Order: Special Victims Unit." The episode, titled "Missing Pieces," which aired just two weeks earlier and was rerun in the Seattle area the night before Sky vanished, depicted a young couple falsely claiming their baby son was abducted when their parked car was stolen, only to later reveal they had buried the boy believing they had accidentally killed him. The eerie parallels between the TV episode and the real-life disappearance of Sky lent a chilling aspect to the investigation, suggesting the possibility that Biryukova might have orchestrated Sky's disappearance as a cover for a more sinister reality.

The perplexing case deepened as investigators and the public scrutinized various aspects of Julia Biryukova's life and actions. Major Mike Johnson of the Bellevue Police Department acknowledged that several members of the command post had noticed a striking resemblance between the circumstances of Sky's disappearance and a recent episode of the TV show "Law & Order:

Special Victims Unit." This revelation was particularly intriguing as Solomon Metalwala, through his attorney, mentioned to the media that "Law & Order" was among his wife's favored TV shows.

Biryukova's digital footprint also became a point of interest. On her Facebook page, an imbalance in her posts raised eyebrows; there were numerous pictures of her daughter Maile, but scarcely any of Sky. This peculiarity in her social media behavior added another layer of intrigue to the ongoing investigation. Additionally, in the months leading up to Sky's disappearance, Biryukova had created a profile on seekingarrangements.com, a dating site typically used by women looking for 'sugar daddies' - affluent men willing to provide financial support within a romantic context. Her profile explicitly stated her desire for "financial stability" and sought monthly financial assistance ranging from $3,000 to $5,000.

Investigators openly expressed skepticism about Biryukova's account of events and harbored suspicions of criminal involvement. Despite this, they stopped short of formally designating her as a prime suspect or a person of interest. Nor did they charge her with child endangerment, despite the nature of the case and her previous arrest (alongside her then-husband) for leaving Sky unattended in a car.

This restraint in bringing charges against Biryukova was later explained as a "strategic decision" by the police. To secure a conviction for child endangerment, it would be necessary to prove that Biryukova did indeed leave Sky alone in the car for an unreasonable amount of time. However, this approach could potentially complicate matters if future evidence suggested a more serious crime, such as murder or kidnapping, possibly involving Biryukova. Arresting her on the lesser charge might impede the prosecution of more severe charges if evidence emerged indicating Sky had never been in the car.

Solomon Metalwala's lawyer provided another rationale for the police's cautious approach. If Biryukova were arrested, she and her legal team would gain access to all the evidence collected by the police up to that point. This was a scenario neither the police nor Solomon desired, as it could potentially reveal the extent of the investigative leads and strategies to Biryukova, potentially impacting the ongoing investigation and any future legal proceedings.

The enigma took a new turn two weeks after the event, when Julia Biryukova finally broke her silence and communicated with the media. ABC News, in a determined effort to gain insights into the case, managed to obtain an email address purportedly belonging to Biryukova from her relatives. Through this channel, they reached out to her. In her response, Biryukova maintained her ignorance about Sky's whereabouts. She also vehemently labeled her ex-husband Solomon as a "sadistic Muslim Pakistani," accusing him of dishonesty. When questioned about the specifics of the case, such as whether her car had actually run out of gas on the morning of Sky's disappearance, she refrained from commenting, citing her lawyer's advice to not discuss the matter publicly.

The authenticity of the email exchange with Biryukova remained uncertain, as she was reportedly staying with relatives during that period. Solomon, however, upon reviewing the correspondence, remarked that the tone and content seemed consistent with Biryukova's manner of communication, though he suspected she might be attempting to provoke him. The Bellevue police, after reviewing the emails shared by ABC News, found themselves unable to comment directly on them but acknowledged that the information could potentially contribute value to their ongoing investigation.

In a significant development, the Washington State Department of Social and Health Services (DSHS) intervened in the aftermath of Sky's disappearance. The department removed Biryukova's daughter, Maile, from her custody and placed her in foster care. This action was taken amidst the swirling uncertainties and allegations surrounding the case. Meanwhile, Solomon actively sought custody of Maile, leveraging the ongoing divorce court proceedings. His efforts were successful as the court eventually granted him custody, following the removal of the remaining protection order that had been in place.

The case lingered in the public consciousness and law enforcement efforts. In 2015, marking the fourth anniversary of the case, Bellevue's newly appointed police chief, Steve Mylett, made a public appeal to Biryukova, urging her to engage once again with the authorities. In a statement to a local newspaper, Chief Mylett expressed his firm belief that Biryukova was a crucial figure in unraveling the mystery of Sky's whereabouts. Despite the Bellevue Police Department previously acknowledging that they had exhausted all leads, Mylett revealed that Solomon had recently provided them with new, unspecified information that could potentially aid in the investigation. In an effort to reignite public interest and assistance in the search, images of Sky were digitally age-progressed and distributed alongside the original photos, depicting how he might look at that time.

As the fourth anniversary of Sky Metalwala's disappearance approached in 2015, the narrative took yet another twist with revelations about Julia Biryukova's personal life. Reports surfaced that Biryukova had not only remarried in the previous year but also welcomed her third child with her new husband, Alan Morgan, in July. This development prompted the Washington State Department of Social and Health Services (DSHS) to consider intervening, as there were efforts to remove the newborn from Biryukova's care.

The DSHS's concerns were primarily centered around Biryukova's mental health, given her history of OCD diagnosis and multiple hospitalizations. The alarm was initially raised following a complaint from the individual who assisted with the delivery of her third child. Adding complexity to the situation, Morgan, a convicted felon with a troubled past, was also under scrutiny. In a concerning parallel, authorities in Florida had previously removed a child from Morgan's care. Additionally, Biryukova had reported Morgan to the Redmond police for alleged assault shortly after their marriage, leading to a no-contact order. Despite this, she continued to visit him in jail in Issaquah, where he was incarcerated during the birth of their child, using assumed names. Both Biryukova and Morgan provided conflicting statements to investigators regarding their living arrangements and even the paternity of the child, despite Morgan's name being on the birth certificate.

In February 2019, Biryukova appeared in court, testifying that Morgan had violated the no-contact order. During this testimony, she also admitted to being prohibited from being alone with her new son unless supervised. Bellevue police spokesperson Seth Tyler commented on the case, affirming their belief that Biryukova had knowledge of Sky's whereabouts. Following her court appearance, Biryukova remained reticent, refusing to engage with the media.

Two years after her court appearance, in a further entanglement with the law, Biryukova was arrested by the Redmond police on a charge of shoplifting. Despite this additional legal trouble, she continued to maintain her silence regarding Sky's disappearance. On the 10th anniversary of the case, the Bellevue police department made a renewed appeal for information. They released an updated flyer featuring an age-progressed image of Sky, now depicted as a 12-year-old. The Bellevue police reiterated their request for Biryukova to cooperate, highlighting the extensive resources invested in the investigation over the past decade, including $2.5 million in expenditures and following up on over 2,500 tips.

Despite extensive searches in the neighborhoods around the area where Julia Biryukova had parked her car, no trace of Sky was ever found. The police maintained a firm belief that Sky did not simply wander away by himself, fueling theories that suggested a more sinister explanation.

With no breakthroughs in the investigation and considering the persistent doubts surrounding Biryukova's account, suspicion increasingly pointed towards her possible involvement in Sky's disappearance. The prevailing theories speculated that if Sky was indeed still alive, Biryukova might have orchestrated for someone else to take him, either on the day she claimed the car ran out of gas or at an earlier time, with the story of him being in the car fabricated. Leslie Clay Berry, the attorney representing Solomon Metalwala, Sky's father, expressed skepticism about Biryukova's version of events in an interview with the Seattle Weekly in 2013. Berry suggested that after realizing her hospital story wasn't gaining traction, Biryukova sought legal counsel.

Solomon Metalwala himself clung to the hope that Sky was still alive, though possibly not in the United States. He recalled that in the spring of 2011, following a doctor's visit that marked the last independently verified sighting of Sky, Biryukova's estranged father had visited from Ukraine. Solomon speculated to the Weekly whether the older man might have taken Sky back to Ukraine with him. However, by 2013, Solomon admitted he had no concrete evidence to support this theory.

Berry, reflecting a more definitive stance, expressed her belief that Sky was never in the car on that fateful morning. She also doubted that any incriminating evidence would be found in Biryukova's apartment, given Biryukova's obsessive-compulsive tendencies, which could have led her to meticulously clean and possibly destroy any potential evidence.

In stark contrast to her client's hopeful perspective, Berry harbored a more pessimistic view regarding the outcome of the case. In her 2013 statement, she expressed her belief that Sky was no longer alive. While Solomon found this difficult to accept, Berry speculated that Biryukova could be responsible for Sky's demise, possibly as a result of neglect rather than a premeditated act. This tragic theory, though unconfirmed, reflected the depths of despair and frustration surrounding a case that had, by then, lingered unresolved for several years.

Tara Calico

On the serene, sun-kissed morning of September 20, 1988, the small town of Belen, New Mexico, was about to witness a mystery that would linger in its collective memory for decades. Nineteen-year-old Tara Calico, known for her radiant smile and sprinkling of freckles, embarked on her routine 36-mile bike ride around 9:30 a.m., unaware that this journey would end in an inexplicable disappearance, leaving a void in her family's heart and a perplexing case for law enforcement.

Tara, typically accompanied by her mother on these rides, found herself alone this day. A recent unnerving experience, where her mother felt they were being trailed by a mysterious motorist, had deterred her from joining. Despite her mother's apprehensions and suggestion to carry mace for protection, Tara, embodying the spirit of independence and headstrong youth, declined. She was determined to enjoy her ride, unencumbered by fears and distractions.

Her plan was simple yet well-timed. The ride, lasting about two hours, was slotted perfectly into her day. She humorously told her mother, Patty Doel, to rescue her around noon if she encountered a flat tire and hadn't returned. After all, she had plans to play tennis with her boyfriend at 12:30 p.m., leaving her ample time to complete her cycling ritual.

Tara set out on her journey, taking her mother's distinct neon pink Huffy mountain bike, and began her usual trek along New Mexico State Road 47. Accompanying her were only her beloved Sony Walkman and headphones, along with a cassette tape of her favorite band, Boston, setting the rhythm for her ride.

As the clock ticked past her expected return time, worry crept into Patty's heart. She drove along Tara's usual route, hoping to find her daughter or at least some sign of her. But the roads offered no answers. Returning home without Tara, a sense of dread settled in, prompting Patty to contact the Valencia County Sheriff's Department and report her daughter missing.

The day's light faded, and a chilling discovery was made. Scattered along the roadside were fragments of Tara's Walkman and the Boston cassette tape. But there was no trace of Tara or her neon pink bike. It was as if she had vanished into thin air, leaving behind only fragments of her last moments and a mystery that would haunt the community, challenge investigators, and remain unsolved in the annals of New Mexico's history.

The disappearance of Tara Calico on that fateful September day in 1988 soon evolved into a labyrinth of leads, rumors, and heart-wrenching theories, each more perplexing than the last. As the investigation deepened, a critical piece of information emerged: witnesses reported seeing an older-model, white or light-colored pickup truck with a camper shell haunting the vicinity of New Mexico State Road 47. More disturbingly, they claimed this truck was following Tara closely on her return journey, casting a sinister shadow over her last known movements.

The narrative took an even more unsettling turn when some witnesses implicated the 18-year-old son of a prominent local law enforcement officer as the passenger in the ominous truck. This revelation sent ripples through the community, intertwining the case with local power dynamics and adding layers of complexity to the investigation.

In 2008, two decades after Tara's disappearance, Valencia Sheriff Rene Rivera broke his silence on the case. He revealed that multiple witnesses had described a harrowing scene: two young men in the truck, allegedly including the officer's son, aggressively pursuing Tara. They were seen trying to engage her, reaching out towards her, and in a tragic turn, the truck collided with Tara's bike, sending her crashing to the ground. According to Rivera, it was at this point that these individuals abducted Tara, a moment that marked the beginning of an enduring mystery.

The saga continued to unfold with grim revelations. In November 2013, a chilling police report surfaced, containing a dying confession from a witness. This individual implicated three men, including the aforementioned officer's son, in the abduction and subsequent disposal of Tara. The report detailed that Tara's bike was discarded in a Belen junkyard, while her body was callously thrown into a pond.

But the torment for Tara's family didn't end there. There were harrowing whispers that Tara had suffered a brutal fate—raped, stabbed to death, and her body concealed beneath concrete slabs. Another gruesome tale suggested her body was hidden in a freezer. Each of these narratives, unsubstantiated but deeply disturbing, added to the profound grief and trauma of Tara's parents.

In an effort to uncover the truth, police conducted exhaustive searches, excavating numerous potential gravesites across Belen and Valencia County. Yet, these efforts yielded no tangible results, leaving the mystery of Tara Calico unsolved.

Adding to the enigma, an article in the Albuquerque Journal disclosed a tragic end for the 21-year-old son of the officer implicated in Tara's disappearance. He died in 1991, in circumstances described as either a suicide or a fatal mishap during a game of Russian roulette. However, the young man's father, embroiled in the web of suspicion surrounding the case, maintained that his son had been murdered, suggesting yet another layer of complexity in this tangled case.

On an ordinary summer day, June 15, 1989, in the quaint town of Port St. Joe, Florida, a discovery was made that would ripple through the nation, stirring intrigue and fear. In the parking lot of a local convenience store, a Polaroid photograph was found, depicting a haunting scene that would etch itself into the public consciousness. Captured within its frame were two individuals – a young woman and a little boy – bound and gagged, their expressions etched with unmistakable distress.

The photograph itself was in remarkably good condition, despite its chilling content. It revealed the two victims tied with their arms behind their backs, their mouths sealed with duct tape. They were positioned in the back of a van, their eyes meeting the camera with a silent plea that spoke volumes. The immediate sense of urgency and the mystery of their identities sparked a swift investigation.

Upon examining the photograph, police sought the expertise of Polaroid executives. The company's analysis indicated a crucial piece of evidence – the picture must have been taken after May 1989. This conclusion was based on the type of film used; it was a stock not available before that date, pinpointing a narrow window for when the disturbing image could have been captured.

The woman who stumbled upon the photograph recalled specific details that would shape the early course of the investigation. She described a windowless, white Toyota cargo van, parked in the lot just moments before her arrival. Notably, she remembered seeing a man, likely in his thirties, with a mustache, who was associated with the van.

In 1989, Port St. Joe was a small, close-knit community, home to just 10,000 residents. The town's size only amplified the shockwaves sent by the photograph's discovery. Local police, in a bid to track down the mysterious mustached man, established roadblocks. Despite these efforts, the man eluded identification, becoming a ghost in a story that was rapidly gaining national attention.

The photograph soon transcended local news, capturing the nation's attention. It was broadcast on the popular television show "A Current Affair" in July 1989, propelling the case into the spotlight. This exposure led to an unexpected connection when Patty Doel, still grappling with the disappearance of her daughter Tara Calico, was contacted by friends who had seen the show. They were struck by a haunting possibility – the girl in the photograph bore a resemblance to Tara.

The enigmatic Polaroid photograph found in Port St. Joe, Florida, quickly became a nexus of hope and heartbreak for families grappling with the pain of missing loved ones. Among them were the relatives of Michael Henley, a 9-year-old boy who had been missing since April 1988 from New Mexico, the same state as Tara Calico. The airing of the photograph on the television show "A Current Affair" sparked a glimmer of recognition among Michael's family, who believed the little boy in the image bore a striking resemblance to Michael.

This development brought the families of Tara and Michael together in a meeting with detectives, united by the hope that the photograph might offer a clue to their children's whereabouts. Patty Doel, Tara's mother, emerged from the meeting convinced that the young woman in the photograph was indeed her daughter. Her conviction was fueled by distinct details: a visible scar on the leg of the woman in the photo, mirroring an injury Tara had suffered in a car accident. Adding to this was the presence of a paperback book, "My Sweet Audrina" by V.C. Andrews, lying next to the woman. This detail was particularly poignant, as Andrews was Tara's favorite author.

The photograph's authenticity and the identities of those it captured became subjects of intense scrutiny and analysis. Scotland Yard delved into the mystery, ultimately concluding that the woman in the photograph was Tara. However, this finding was met with conflicting opinions, as a second analysis by the Los Alamos National Laboratory disagreed with Scotland Yard's assessment. The FBI also conducted an analysis but could only offer an inconclusive verdict, further deepening the mystery.

The case took a heartbreaking turn with developments regarding Michael Henley. Michael had vanished while on a turkey hunting trip with his father in the New Mexico wilderness, approximately 75 miles from Tara's abduction site. His parents, initially convinced that their son was the boy in the Polaroid, faced a tragic reality. In June 1990, Michael's remains were discovered in the Zuni Mountains, about seven miles from where he had disappeared. This discovery rendered it highly unlikely that Michael was the boy in the photograph, dashing the family's hopes and leaving more questions than answers.

Another name emerged in the swirl of theories surrounding the Polaroid – David Borer. David vanished on April 26, 1989, in Willow, Alaska. Last seen walking towards Mile Marker 82 on Parks Highway, a short distance north of his hometown, David's destination was believed to be either a friend's home or a sandbar at the Kashwitna River. Despite extensive searches, no conclusive evidence was found at the river. Search dogs tracked David's scent to Parks Highway, but from there, the trail went cold. The absence of clear signs and the circumstances surrounding his disappearance led the police to not rule out foul play. To this day, David Borer remains missing.

The haunting saga only deepened with the emergence of additional photographs over the years. Each image brought with it a renewed wave of hope and dread for Tara's family, who found themselves caught in a relentless cycle of hope and despair, trying to discern if these photographs held the key to unraveling Tara's fate.

The first of these new photographs was discovered in a location far removed from the initial mystery - near a construction site in Montecito, California. This image presented a blurry yet unsettling scene: a girl's face, her mouth obscured by tape, set against a backdrop of light blue striped fabric. This detail chillingly mirrored the pillow seen in the original photograph found in the Toyota van. Notably, the film used for this photograph was not available until June 1989, aligning with the timeline of Tara's disappearance.

The second photograph surfaced under equally mysterious circumstances, depicting a woman bound in gauze, her eyes peering out from behind large, black-framed glasses. Beside her, an unidentified male figure. This image, captured on a different type of film stock, was traced back to no earlier than February 1990.

For Tara's mother, the agony of these discoveries was palpable. She believed that the girl with the striped fabric could indeed be Tara, a conviction that must have reignited a mix of hope and torment. However, she harbored doubts about the second photo, suspecting it might be a distasteful prank.

Tara's sister, Michelle, approached these developments with a guarded perspective. "They had a striking resemblance," she admitted, acknowledging the haunting possibility that these images could be connected to her sister. Yet, she also recognized the emotional toll of this process, having faced the daunting task of identifying numerous other photographs over the years, most of which were eventually ruled out.

The mystery took another bizarre turn in 2009 when Port St. Joe Police Chief David Barnes received two mysterious envelopes, postmarked from Albuquerque, New Mexico. The first envelope contained a photograph printed on standard copy paper. It depicted a young boy, his mouth obscured by a crudely drawn black ink band, eerily reminiscent of the gag in the 1989 photograph. The second envelope held an image of the same boy, this time without the inked gag.

But the peculiar correspondence did not end there. In August of the same year, the Star newspaper in Port St. Joe received a third letter, again mailed from Albuquerque. It included the same image of the boy, once more with the black marker gag over his mouth. Notably, none of these letters offered a return address or any clue as to the child's identity.

Patty Doel, in her later years, was particularly haunted by Tara's absence. Suffering from health setbacks, including several strokes, she spent her days in a Florida retirement home alongside her husband, John. There, Patty's vigil for Tara continued, her gaze often fixed on the world outside her window. In every cyclist that passed by, she saw a glimpse of Tara, a mirage of hope in the ordinary ebb and flow of life. This heartbreaking ritual was a testament to a mother's unwavering love and the pain of unresolved loss.

John Doel, reflecting on those years after Patty's passing in 2006, recounted the painful reality of trying to gently bring his wife back from her hopeful visions. "Patty was looking for Tara right to the end," he said, a poignant reminder of the deep scars left by Tara's disappearance.

Patty and John Doel had been the pillars of the search for Tara, driven by a relentless determination to find their daughter. Their dedication led them to become deputized, empowering them to conduct their own searches and distribute thousands of flyers nationwide. Patty's appearances on national television shows were not just efforts to find Tara, but also resonated as a mother's plea for answers, a voice for the missing.

In 2013, years after Patty's passing, the Albuquerque Journal reported a renewed effort in the investigation. A six-person task force, comprising local and federal law enforcement officers, was formed to reexamine Tara's case, indicating that the quest for answers was far from over. However, the task force was disbanded a year later, leaving many questions unanswered.

Decades after Tara's disappearance, in September 2021, there was a glimmer of progress. Lt. Joseph Rowland of the Valencia County Sheriff's Office announced that new leads had emerged, leading to the execution of a search warrant at a home in Valencia County. The specifics of this warrant, including the nature of the leads and the findings of the search, remain shrouded in secrecy, adding another layer of mystery to the case.

In a groundbreaking development, June 2023 marked a significant moment in the investigation. The Valencia County Sheriff's Office, under the leadership of Sheriff Denise Vigil, held a press conference to announce a suspect in the Tara Calico case. While details about the suspect's identity and the nature of the evidence were kept under wraps, Sheriff Vigil conveyed a sense of cautious hope. "I personally was not sure I would ever see the day of a significant breakthrough, but here we are today," she said, her words reflecting both the long journey of the case and the potential for closure that still lies ahead.

Lauren Spierer

auren Spierer's life story is both intriguing and heartrending. Born on January 17, 1991, in the prosperous community of Scarsdale, New York, Lauren was the cherished daughter of Charlene and Robert Spierer. Her father, a dedicated accountant, and her mother provided a nurturing home in this affluent suburb of Westchester County. Lauren's early years were marked by a typical suburban upbringing, filled with the joys and challenges of growing up in a close-knit community.

A bright and ambitious student, Lauren graduated from Edgemont High School in 2009. She then embarked on a new chapter in her life at Indiana University, where she pursued her passion for textiles merchandising. This choice of study was a testament to her creativity and interest in the fashion industry.

Lauren's involvement in the Jewish community at Indiana University was a significant aspect of her college life. She was deeply committed to her faith and cultural heritage, exemplified by her participation in activities like planting trees in Israel during a spring break, a venture organized by the Jewish National Fund. These experiences not only enriched her personal growth but also strengthened her ties to her community.

The story of how Lauren met her boyfriend, Jesse Wolff, and her friend, Jay Rosenbaum, takes us back to her younger days at Camp Towanda. This summer camp, nestled in the mountainous region of Honesdale, Pennsylvania, was a place of fun, friendship, and discovery. It was here that Lauren formed lasting bonds with Jesse, Jay, and other future Indiana University students, who would later become an integral part of her social circle at college.

Lauren's disappearance is a poignant and mysterious chapter in her life. On the fateful night, she was out socializing with friends, a typical college experience tinged with youthful exuberance. Jesse Wolff, her boyfriend, shared that he wasn't with Lauren and her friends that evening, staying in touch with her through text messages before retiring for the night. The circumstances of that night were further complicated by witness accounts of Lauren's noticeable intoxication.

The Bloomington police pieced together the events leading up to Lauren's disappearance, using video surveillance footage and witness statements to create a detailed timeline. Her whereabouts before she vanished were scrutinized in an effort to unravel the mystery of what happened to Lauren Spierer.

The night of Friday, June 3, 2011, unfolded like a complex tapestry of events, leading to the mysterious disappearance of Lauren Spierer. Each moment, captured by surveillance and recounted by witnesses, adds a piece to the puzzle.

The evening began at 12:30 a.m., with Spierer leaving her apartment accompanied by a friend named David Rohn. Their destination was Jay Rosenbaum's apartment, where Spierer was soon to meet Corey Rossman, Rosenbaum's neighbor. Little did they know that these moments would become crucial pieces of a larger, unresolved mystery.

At 1:46 a.m., the vibrant energy of Kilroy's Sports Bar welcomed Spierer. The cameras there caught her entering, a seemingly innocuous moment that would later be scrutinized for any clue to her fate. It was here, at 2:27 a.m., that Spierer was last seen leaving the bar with Rossman. Notably, she left behind her cell phone and shoes, a decision spurred by the comfort of the bar's sand-covered patio.

The next timestamp, at 2:30 a.m., showed Spierer entering the Smallwood Plaza apartments. This is where a concerned passerby, Zach Oakes, noticed her apparent level of inebriation and questioned her well-being. These fleeting interactions added layers to the growing concern for her safety.

By 2:48 a.m., the night took a more mysterious turn. Spierer was seen entering an alley between College Avenue and Morton Street. The security cameras captured her emerging from the alley at 2:51 a.m., walking towards an empty lot. Disturbingly, it was along this route that her keys and purse were later found.

The narrative continued at Rossman's apartment, where Spierer and Rossman arrived shortly after. Here, Michael Beth, Rossman's roommate, recounted Rossman's extreme intoxication. Beth's attempt to care for both, by trying to get Spierer to stay over for safety and putting Rossman to bed, highlighted the concerning state of affairs.

The timeline progressed to 3:30 a.m., with Beth contacting their neighbor, Rosenbaum, to look after Spierer. Despite Beth's insistence, Spierer seemed determined to return to her own apartment. At Rosenbaum's apartment, a new detail emerged - a bruise under Spierer's eye, its origin unknown to her. Rosenbaum recalled Spierer making two phone calls, both unanswered, adding to the aura of concern.

The last known sighting of Spierer was at 4:30 a.m., as reported by Rosenbaum. He last saw her at the intersection of 11th Street and College Avenue, heading south. Her appearance was notable: barefoot, in black leggings and a white shirt, a stark image against the backdrop of a quiet college town.

In the following hours, a text message from her boyfriend, Jesse Wolff, would only be replied to by an employee at the bar, a chilling indication that something was amiss. It was then that Wolff reported Spierer missing, marking the start of a heartrending journey for answers that continues to this day.

In August 2011, a substantial nine-day search operation was launched at the Sycamore Ridge Landfill in Pimento, a location south of Terre Haute. This particular landfill was a focal point as it is the final destination for trash from Bloomington, following an intermediate stop at a transfer station. This meticulous search was a joint effort involving multiple law enforcement agencies, including the Bloomington Police Department, the Indiana University Police Department, and the FBI. The commitment to uncovering clues in this perplexing case was evident, as by May 24, 2013, investigators had painstakingly sifted through a staggering 3,060 tips related to Spierer's disappearance, with a notable 100 of these tips emerging in the first half of 2013 alone.

The plot thickened in April 2015 when the Bloomington Police announced an investigation into a potential connection between Spierer's disappearance and the tragic murder of another Indiana University student, Hannah Wilson. Wilson's case bore eerie similarities to that of Spierer's. She went missing on April 24, 2015, after a night at Kilroy's, the same bar Spierer had visited on the night she vanished. The last sighting of Wilson was her getting into a taxi outside the bar, and tragically, her body was discovered the following morning in Brown County. The arrest of Daniel Messel for Wilson's murder, spurred by the discovery of his cell phone near Wilson's body, added a chilling dimension to the investigation. However, by July 2015, authorities concluded that the two cases were unrelated, attributing any similarities to mere coincidence.

The investigation took another turn on January 28, 2016, when the FBI, along with other police agencies, descended upon a property on Old Morgantown Road in Martinsville, located roughly 20 miles north of Bloomington. This operation was part of a concerted effort to follow up on leads related to

Spierer's disappearance in Morgan County. The property under scrutiny belonged to a man named Justin Wagers, who lived there with his mother and stepfather. Wagers had come under suspicion for separate incidents involving indecent exposure to local women.

During the search of this property, investigators deployed cadaver dogs, which signaled the potential presence of evidence. Anthropologists were brought in to conduct a thorough dig and sift through the soil in the barn where the dogs had indicated, but, disappointingly, no conclusive evidence was found. Additionally, a white truck belonging to Wagers was towed from the property.

The enigma surrounding Lauren Spierer's disappearance has given rise to a multitude of theories, each delving into various aspects of that fateful evening. The anguish and determination of Spierer's parents have been central to this narrative. They have publicly expressed their heart-wrenching belief that their daughter is no longer alive. This belief is partly rooted in the details surrounding her level of intoxication on the night she vanished. Robert Spierer, Lauren's father, conveyed their suspicion that she might have been drugged at Kilroy's bar, suggesting the possibility of foul play.

A significant focus of the family's suspicion has been on the individuals Spierer was last seen with, including her friend Wolff. The family's distress is compounded by the fact that these men declined to participate in police-issued polygraph tests and sought legal representation shortly after Lauren's disappearance. While the Spierers have refrained from outright accusations, they firmly believe that these individuals hold more information than they have disclosed to the authorities. In response, the men have indicated that they have undergone privately administered polygraphs, as well as one by the FBI, and their decision to retain lawyers was motivated by a lack of trust in the Bloomington police.

Among the theories is the possibility of an accidental overdose. Friends and Wolff told police that Spierer had consumed drugs in addition to alcohol on the night she disappeared. Allegations about her past drug use, including an incident at a summer camp and a previous arrest for public intoxication and illegal consumption, have been brought to light. After her disappearance, a small amount of cocaine was found in her room. Rosenbaum, one of the last people to see Spierer, told investigators about her consumption of alcohol, cocaine, and crushed Klonopin tablets. Her pre-existing rare heart condition, long QT syndrome, made this combination particularly dangerous. This has led to speculations that Spierer might have overdosed, and those with her, fearing legal repercussions, may have concealed her body. However, Bo Dietl, a private investigator hired by the Spierer family, doubts this theory, citing widespread drug use on the IU campus and questioning whether it would be sufficient motive to hide her death.

Another angle considered by the police is the possibility of stranger abduction, although Spierer's parents have previously expressed doubts about this scenario being the case for their daughter.

An intriguing twist emerged in 2017 when Brown County prosecutor Ted Adams suggested a potential connection between Daniel Messel and Spierer's case. Messel was convicted in 2016 for the murder of Hannah Wilson, another IU student whose body was found in a desolate field, having been bludgeoned to death. The discovery of Messel's cell phone near Wilson's body added a chilling layer to this theory. Despite these suspicions, Messel has not been charged in relation to Spierer's disappearance.

Spierer's parents embarked on a legal battle against Rossman, Rosenbaum, and Beth, who were with Lauren on the night leading up to her disappearance. They filed civil lawsuits, charging these individuals with negligence. The core of their argument was that these men supplied an already visibly intoxicated Lauren with more alcohol and then failed to ensure her safe return to her apartment, actions they believe directly contributed to her tragic fate.

The Spierer family's motivation for pursuing legal action went beyond seeking justice; they harbored a deep-seated hope that the lawsuit would compel the defendants to reveal more about the events of that fateful night. Lauren's mother poignantly expressed her belief that her daughter's disappearance was not a random act but rather the result of actions by someone Lauren knew. In an aggressive legal strategy, the family subpoenaed extensive private records of the defendants, including cell phone and academic details, covering a period of 134 days before and after Lauren's disappearance. This move was criticized by the defendants' lawyers as a broad and unfocused "fishing expedition."

The legal journey faced significant setbacks. In 2013, federal judge Tanya Walton Pratt dismissed the lawsuit against Beth, citing a lack of duty of care towards Spierer. This was a significant blow to the family's quest for answers.

The legal challenges continued in 2014 when Judge Pratt also dismissed the suit against Rossman and Rosenbaum. She reasoned that, given the myriad of theories about what happened to Lauren and the absence of concrete evidence to support these theories, it was impossible for a jury to determine if her disappearance was a direct consequence of her intoxication or if other intervening factors played a role. The Spierer family, undeterred, appealed this ruling, but their efforts met with further disappointment as the dismissal was upheld by a federal appeals court in 2015.

Throughout this process, the lawyers representing the men have maintained that their clients have been nothing but cooperative with both the police and the private investigators hired by the Spierer family. They assert that their clients have been thoroughly interviewed multiple times and have passed private polygraph tests. The defense attorneys emphasize that portraying these men as uncooperative is misleading. As of now, none of the defendants have been officially named as suspects in the mysterious and haunting disappearance of Lauren Spierer.

The Missing Fort Worth Trio

On a chilly morning on December 23, 1974, in the bustling city of Fort Worth, Texas, an ordinary day took an extraordinary turn for three young girls - Lisa Renee Wilson, Julie Ann Moseley, and Mary Rachel Trlica. The air was filled with the festive spirit as the trio set out for a day of Christmas shopping at the popular Seminary South Shopping Center. Lisa and Mary, who preferred to be called by their middle names, Renee and Rachel respectively, shared a close friendship, while Julie, the younger sister of Renee's boyfriend, Terry Moseley, eagerly joined them on this adventure.

The day's plan had originally included Terry, but a change in his schedule to visit a friend in the hospital altered the course of events. Julie, feeling left out at home and yearning for companionship, pleaded with her mother, Rayanne, for permission to tag along with the older girls. After a bit of persuasion highlighting her loneliness at home, Julie received the green light, with one firm condition - she had to be home by 6:00 pm. This arrangement seemed perfect, as Renee also had plans to attend a Christmas party with Terry later that evening and aimed to be home by 4:00 pm to prepare.

Their journey began at noon, with their first stop being an Army/Navy surplus store to pick up a pair of jeans Renee had on layaway. Spirits high and laughter in the air, they then proceeded to the Seminary South Shopping Center. Rachel's 1974 Oldsmobile 98 found its spot in the upper parking level, conveniently close to the Sears outlet.

As the day unfolded, various witnesses reported seeing the girls meandering through the mall, their arms gradually filling with the spoils of their shopping spree. It's believed that at some point, they made their way back to the Oldsmobile to offload their purchases. However, it was from this point on that the narrative took a mysterious turn.

As nightfall approached on December 23, 1974, and the vibrant lights of the Seminary South Shopping Center in Fort Worth, Texas, began to twinkle, a sense of unease and dread started to creep into the hearts of three families. The joyful anticipation of the return of Lisa Renee Wilson, Julie Ann Moseley, and Mary Rachel Trlica from their Christmas shopping excursion transformed into deep concern when the girls failed to make their way home. In a desperate bid to locate them, their anxious families embarked on a frantic search, converging on the shopping center that had been the girls' last known location.

Terry Moseley, caught in a tumult of worry for his sister Julie and his girlfriend Renee, was assigned a critical role in the search efforts – to remain at home, vigilantly by the phone, awaiting any call that might shed light on the whereabouts of the missing girls.

The first tangible clue in this bewildering puzzle surfaced around 6:00 pm when Rachel's Oldsmobile was located in the parking lot. The car, locked and seemingly undisturbed, held a solitary present on the backseat floorboard, an eerie reminder of the day's festive beginnings. A thorough examination of the vehicle revealed no signs of a struggle, nor any clue as to the girls' fate.

As the hours ticked by, the families' vigil intensified. Renee's mother, Judy Wilson, spearheaded a meticulous search, having the girls' names paged through each store's intercom system, while simultaneously reaching out to local hospitals and law enforcement. Rusty Arnold, Julie's brother, along with their mother, combed through the shopping center, store by store, hoping for any sign of the girls.

In a display of determination and guardianship, Richard Wilson, Renee's father, accompanied by a neighbor, took to the roof of a nearby building. Armed with a shotgun, they kept a protective watch over the Oldsmobile, a silent sentinel in the sprawling parking lot.

Meanwhile, a network of phone calls was initiated, reaching out to each of the girls' friends, desperately seeking any information. But the night yielded no answers; the friends had heard nothing. With each passing hour, hope waned, and the situation grew increasingly dire.

Recognizing the gravity of the situation, the families notified the police. The case quickly escalated, drawing the focused attention of the Fort Worth Police Department's Missing Persons Bureau, specifically its youth division. As the community of Fort Worth held its breath, a dedicated team of investigators began piecing together the scant clues, embarking on a search that would soon capture the attention of a nation and become one of the most haunting and enduring mysteries of the time.

From the outset, law enforcement officers clung to the theory that the girls had voluntarily run away. This assumption, vehemently contested by the families of the missing girls, significantly impacted the initial stages of the investigation. Crucial forensic opportunities, such as processing Mary Rachel's car for evidence or dusting for fingerprints, were overlooked, as the case wasn't given the gravity and urgency it demanded during its critical first year.

This theory of voluntary disappearance gained unwarranted traction when a curious piece of correspondence entered the narrative. On the morning of December 24, 1974, just a day after the girls' disappearance, Rachel's husband, Thomas, discovered a peculiar letter in their mailbox. Addressed to him from "Rachel," the letter, penned on a sheet of paper awkwardly wider than the envelope, conveyed a hasty message. It claimed that the girls had impulsively decided to journey to Houston for a week and provided directions to the mall parking lot where Mary Rachel's car was parked. The tone of the letter, reading, "I know I'm going to catch it, but we just had to get away," seemed uncharacteristically frivolous given the gravity of their disappearance.

This hastily written note, described as a "childish scrawl," bore a stamp that had been canceled the morning it arrived. However, the envelope's postmark was a puzzle in itself, marked only by a blurry Postal Service number, "76083," with the "3" peculiarly printed backwards. This oddity led to speculation about the postmark's origin, ranging from Eliasville or Throckmorton if the number was indeed "76083," or Weatherford, Texas, if interpreted as "76088."

Further deepening the mystery, the letter's authenticity was called into question by Rachel's mother and Thomas. Rachel commonly referred to her husband affectionately as "Tommy," not the formal "Thomas A. Trlica" used in the letter. Handwriting analysis yielded inconclusive results, leaving the authorship a matter of debate. Intriguingly, a closer examination of the letter revealed that the loop in the "L" of "Rachel" appeared to have been initially an 'e,' hinting at a possible correction from an erroneous spelling.

This enigmatic letter stands as the solitary piece of tangible evidence in this confounding case. With the advent of DNA technology, the letter was subjected to forensic analysis, yet it failed to match any profiles in the police database or provide a direct connection to the missing girls.

Amidst the swirling mysteries, another intriguing subplot involved Rachel's sister, Debra, who was living with Rachel and Thomas at the time of the disappearance. The dynamics of this living arrangement were peculiar, given Thomas and Debra's past engagement, which had been called off without much fanfare. Despite the potential for discomfort, both Thomas and Debra maintained that their cohabitation with Rachel was unproblematic.

A notable suspicion arose within some members of the Moseley, Wilson, and Arnold families regarding Debra Arnold's possible knowledge about the case.

This suspicion was further fueled following an interview Debra gave to the Fort Worth-Star Telegram in 2000. In response, the families penned a letter to her, appealing for any information she might possess. They implored Debra to engage fully with the investigations led by the Fort Worth Police Department and the FBI and requested her participation in a polygraph test, hoping to glean new insights into the baffling case. Despite these efforts, Debra has consistently maintained her lack of knowledge about the girls' fate.

Amidst the growing despair and frustration, the families remained relentless in their search for answers. They embarked on a widespread campaign, distributing missing persons flyers across Texas and reaching out to newspapers nationwide to amplify the mystery of the disappearances.

The case took various intriguing turns as witnesses came forward with pieces of information, albeit unverified. A store clerk at the mall reported a troubling account of a woman claiming to have seen Renee, Rachel, and Julie being forcefully taken into a yellow pickup truck near Buddies grocery store on the day they vanished. This account echoed a similar, earlier report from 1981, where a witness claimed to have seen an unidentified male coercing a girl, or possibly multiple girls, into a van in the mall's parking lot. Despite the alarming nature of these reports, police were unable to corroborate these stories or trace the woman who spoke to the cashier.

Investigators also explored leads that emerged from unexpected sources. A night watchman at Alcon Laboratories, located near the shopping center, reported witnessing a car with three women and two men entering the building's driveway on the night of the disappearances, but this lead eventually hit a dead end. Another intriguing claim came from a ticket agent at the local bus depot, who reported that three girls had inquired about trips to Houston and other destinations the morning after the trio's disappearance. However, the reliability of this information remained uncertain.

In a turn towards the unconventional, the families enlisted the help of a well-known psychic, J. Joseph, who offered his services without charge and contributed to the growing reward fund. Joseph's involvement brought a mix of mystique and somber predictions to the case. He expressed doubts about the authenticity of the letter purportedly sent by Rachel and claimed to sense that the girls had been taken north towards Oklahoma or Illinois. His grim assertions suggested that they were being held against their will, possibly in connection with drugs, and involving three to five individuals. In a particularly eerie and foreboding statement made at the Arnold home, he implied that his future absence would signal the girls' demise. True to his ominous message, Joseph never again made contact with the families.

In 1975, the investigation took a notable turn when a man, claiming to be an acquaintance of Rachel's, provided a potential lead. He recounted seeing the three girls at a record store within the mall mere hours before their mysterious disappearance. His account included a detail that caught the investigators' attention: the presence of an additional individual in the company of the girls, and a brief interaction he had with Mary.

Around the same time, in the town of Justin, Texas, a discovery momentarily raised hopes. A collection of women's clothing was found, initially suspected to be connected to one of the missing girls. However, after thorough examination, it was concluded that these items bore no relation to the case, dashing the fleeting hopes of the families and investigators.

Frustrated with the police's handling of the investigation, the families took a decisive step in 1975 by hiring private investigator Jon Swaim. Swaim's involvement marked a shift in the case's trajectory. He held numerous press conferences, applying pressure on the police to grant him access to their case files. His proactive approach gained national attention, particularly when an incident involving an unidentified individual attempting to claim the reward money with false information about the girls' whereabouts came to light under his watch.

In April 1975, following a tip, Swaim led a substantial search operation in Port Lavaca, Texas. Accompanied by a group of 100 volunteers, they scoured beneath local bridges, acting on information suggesting that the bodies of the girls might be found there. Despite the city having been previously searched by investigators with no results, Swaim's team persisted, only to find their efforts yield the same outcome.

Swaim's investigation uncovered various leads, including the unsettling activities of a 28-year-old man in August of that year. This individual, employed at a local store where Rachel had once applied for a job, had lived in her neighborhood and was involved in making obscene phone calls in the area. Although this lead did not directly advance the case, it exposed the man's predatory behavior, as he had used his position to gather personal information from young female applicants, leading to a series of disturbing phone calls.

In 1976, a grim discovery by an oil drilling crew in Brazoria County, Texas momentarily captured the attention of the investigation. Three skeletons were unearthed in a field, prompting Swaim to have them compared against the missing girls' x-rays and dental records. However, the remains were identified as belonging to one male, aged between 15 and 17, and two other females, none of whom matched the profiles of Renee, Julie, and Rachel.

Swaim's involvement in the case came to an abrupt and tragic end in 1979 when he died by apparent suicide. In a final, enigmatic act, he requested the destruction of all his records upon his death, leaving unanswered whether these files contained any significant leads or breakthroughs in the unsolved case of the missing Fort Worth trio.

Renee's parents were forced to acquire a second phone line due to the constant barrage of calls from individuals falsely claiming to be their missing daughter, adding an excruciating layer of emotional turmoil to their already unbearable situation.

In 1999, in an effort to reinvigorate the search, Rachel's brother, Rusty, enlisted the aid of private investigator Dan James. Together, they delved into various witness accounts claiming sightings of Rachel and Renee at different locations, including stores and a gas station, in the days following their disappearance. Additionally, there have been recurring reports of Rachel being spotted in the Fort Worth area, particularly during several Christmas seasons, sparking a flicker of hope that she might still be alive.

Rusty and James have come to the somber conclusion that Renee and Julie are likely no longer alive. However, they hold onto the belief that Rachel might still be alive, based on the aforementioned sightings. They suspect that unknown individuals are preventing her from returning to her family. Despite their strong convictions, they have been reticent about revealing any concrete evidence to support these claims.

In a significant move in December 1999, James announced a $25,000 reward from his personal savings for information leading to the arrest and conviction of those responsible for the girls' disappearances. His commitment to the case extends beyond financial contributions; he is also a sponsor of the website missingtrio.com, which provides updates and information about the investigation. Despite not receiving any financial compensation for his investigative work, James has remained dedicated to the cause.

James' involvement in the case has not been without personal risk. He has reported receiving death threats from anonymous callers, demanding that he withdraw from the investigation, a testament to the potential dangers and complexities surrounding the case.

In a renewed effort to solve this enduring mystery, the case was officially reopened by investigators in January 2001. A few months later, in April 2001, a press conference was held, revealing that at least 20 new witnesses had been interviewed. These witnesses reported seeing the girls at the mall on the afternoon of their disappearance. The investigators also announced that they had narrowed down their list of suspects to five individuals.

Adding another intriguing twist to the case, in the same month, a former Fort Worth policeman and security guard at the Seminary South Sears outlet came forward with a significant claim. Speaking to news station KXAS NBC-5, he recounted seeing three girls and a young male security guard in a pickup truck around 11:30 pm on the night they vanished. According to his observation, the girls seemed relaxed and were engaged in conversation and laughter with the security guard before driving away. He detailed the seating arrangement in the truck, noting the youngest girl sat next to the driver, with the other two positioned accordingly.

The former policeman had reportedly contacted the police soon after the girls' disappearance became public, but it wasn't until April 2001 that the investigators actively followed up on his information. When media outlets reached out to the investigators, they revealed that they had located and questioned the security guard mentioned by the witness, only to have him deny that the girls were ever in his vehicle that night.

Over the years, the families have endured the emotional turmoil of receiving reports claiming that the bodies of the missing girls have been found, only to have their hopes dashed when none of these remains were identified as belonging to Renee, Julie, or Rachel. The search has extended beyond Texas, with investigators even scouring state medical examiner records in New Mexico for unidentified females, but to no avail. In preparation for the possibility of a grim discovery, the dental records and DNA profiles of the trio are on file for comparison.

In a notable effort in September 2018, Rusty Arnold, driven by a relentless pursuit of closure, teamed up with Texas EquuSearch to retrieve two submerged cars from Benbrook Lake. This initiative was spurred by information about an individual who lived near the mall and had a vehicle that went missing in the mid-1970s. Despite the lake's proximity to the shopping center and the intriguing nature of this lead, investigators did not deem it sufficient to conduct an official search, prompting Rusty to take matters into his own hands. A GoFundMe campaign was launched to finance the recovery operation, which involved divers from North Texas Marine Salvage and specialized equipment.

The first car was recovered on September 22, 2018, followed by the second on October 13. A team of five scientists was brought in to examine these vehicles. Although the analysis of their VIN numbers and other features did not link them to the case of the missing girls, the information was retained in case it might be relevant to other unsolved cases in the area.

Rusty's investigation also led to the discovery of a third car submerged in Benbrook Lake. Plans to retrieve it were ultimately abandoned due to the deteriorated condition of the vehicle, making the operation too perilous.

In an effort to encourage public assistance in solving this enduring mystery, Crime Stoppers has offered a $1,000 reward for information leading to a resolution in the case.

One particularly heart-wrenching moment for the families occurred when Rusty received a call from a woman who believed she might be Julie. Having seen a photograph of Julie online and harboring doubts about her own past, she reached out to Rusty. Both he and Julie's mother briefly entertained the possibility that she could be the missing girl, but their hopes were crushed when a DNA test confirmed otherwise.

The investigation has been marked by sporadic leads and limited revelations. In 2001, investigators collected DNA evidence, but the ongoing nature of the investigation has kept the results confidential. Their prevailing theory is that the girls left the shopping center with someone they trusted, only to meet with foul play.

The lack of transparent details and progress in the investigation has been a source of immense frustration for the families. Richard Wilson, in particular, has voiced his disillusionment. He recounted an instance to FWWeekly where he was led to believe the police were investigating a lead about the girls' bodies being in a well in Aledo, Texas. Following the officers to a Paris Coffee Shop and then back to the station, he later discovered that they had never actually visited the well, a revelation that added to the anguish and disappointment felt by the families.

Through the decades, thousands of leads have been pursued and dozens of searches conducted. Searchers have traversed the rugged Texas terrain, explored remote back roads, while the families themselves have walked tirelessly along creek beds and rural paths, all in the hope of finding a clue, a sign, anything that would bring them a step closer to understanding the fate of Renee, Julie, and Rachel.

Asha Degree

Harold and Iquilla Degree, who tied the knot on the romantic Valentine's Day of 1988, embarked on a journey of love and family. The following year, they welcomed their son O'Bryant into the world, and soon after, in 1990, their daughter Asha joined the family. Nestled in the charming Oakcrest Drive, their home stood in a serene residential subdivision, a picturesque setting amidst the rural expanses north of Shelby, North Carolina. This area, on the cusp of the bustling Charlotte metropolitan zone, offered a tranquil retreat for the Degree family.

The Degrees, both hardworking and dedicated, ensured a stable life for their children. Harold, a committed dock loader, and Iquilla, employed at Kawai America Manufacturing assembling pianos, were the epitome of diligence. Their children, after school, would return to an empty home but one filled with expectations of discipline and academic focus. Their parents, returning later, anticipated completed homework and a sense of responsibility upheld by their offspring.

Asha and O'Bryant grew up in a household that cherished traditional values and was cautious of modern technology's influence. The Degree home was notably devoid of a computer, a decision rooted in Iquilla's concerns about the dangers lurking online, as she vividly described in a 2013 interview with Jet. The internet, in her eyes, was a gateway for malevolent characters to disrupt the innocence of childhood. Asha, in particular, seemed to adapt well to these boundaries. Described as shy and cautious, she rarely stepped outside the limits set by her parents. Even a fear of dogs was a testament to her apprehensive nature, leading Iquilla to believe that Asha would always stay within the safety of their home.

Asha's life, however, wasn't confined to the boundaries of her home. A student at the nearby Fallston Elementary School, she was an active participant in her community. In February 2000, as Asha was in her fourth-grade year, a long weekend loomed ahead. The Cleveland County Schools had declared a holiday on Friday, February 11, but work commitments kept Harold and Iquilla busy. The children spent the day at their aunt's house, within the same neighborhood, a routine day that included attending their youth basketball practices at school.

Basketball was a significant part of Asha's life. A star point guard on her team, she experienced the highs and lows of sports. On a fateful day, following a losing game where she had fouled out, Asha showed a rare display of emotion, shedding tears along with her teammates. Her parents recalled this moment vividly, noting that although she appeared deeply affected, she eventually seemed to recover, even managing to watch her brother's game thereafter.

On February 13, a serene Sunday, the Degree children started their day with a visit to church from a relative's house, a routine that symbolized their deep-rooted family values and faith. As the day unfolded, returning to their home marked the end of a typical weekend. Around 8 p.m., the children retreated to the room they shared, embracing the comfort of their beds, unaware of the extraordinary events that were about to unfold.

The tranquility of the night was abruptly disturbed when, almost an hour later, a nearby car accident caused a power outage that plunged the neighborhood into darkness. The silence of the night was only broken by the occasional rustling of leaves outside. It wasn't until 12:30 a.m. that the electricity flickered back to life, restoring light and a semblance of normalcy. Harold, ever the vigilant father, checked on his children at this time, finding both

Asha and O'Bryant peacefully asleep in their beds. His mind at ease, he went about his late-night routines.

In the early hours of February 14, as Valentine's Day dawned, Harold performed another routine check before retiring at 2:30 a.m. Once again, he saw his children, cocooned in the safety of their beds. But the night was far from over.

Shortly after Harold's last check, O'Bryant, then only 10 years old, was stirred from his sleep by the sound of Asha's bed squeaking. Assuming his sister was merely shifting in her sleep, he drifted back into his own slumber, unaware of the significant turn of events unfolding. Unbeknownst to her family, Asha had silently prepared for a mysterious journey, packing a bookbag with clothes and personal items. In the dead of night, she slipped out of the house, embarking on a path that would soon concern and baffle an entire community.

Between the haunting hours of 3:45 and 4:15 a.m., under the cover of darkness and an impending storm, Asha was spotted walking along Highway 18. Dressed in a white T-shirt and white pants, her figure was a startling sight for a truck driver and a motorist passing by. The uniqueness of a child alone at such an hour prompted the motorist to investigate. Circling three times, he witnessed Asha dart into the woods, vanishing into the night. The storm's intensity added a dramatic backdrop to this mysterious scene. The witnesses later relayed their accounts to the police, correlating closely with Asha's last known appearance.

The morning of February 14 began like any other for Iquilla, who woke at 5:45 a.m. to prepare for the school day. That morning's routine included drawing a bath for the children, a task made necessary by the previous night's power outage. But as she opened the children's room, expecting to rouse them from their slumber, she was met with a heart-dropping discovery. O'Bryant was in his bed, but Asha was nowhere to be seen. A frantic search of the house and family cars ensued, but Asha remained missing. Iquilla's alarm escalated as she informed Harold, who suggested checking with his mother across the street. The absence of Asha at her grandmother's house sent Iquilla into a state of panic. Rushing outside, she was driven by a desperate need to find her daughter. Her next call was to her mother, who advised her to contact the police.

As dawn broke on February 14, the Degree family's quiet neighborhood was disrupted by the sudden arrival of police officers. By 6:40 a.m., the first responders had descended upon the scene, a tangible sense of urgency in the air. The situation was dire: Asha Degree, a young girl, had vanished into the night, leaving behind a trail of confusion and worry. The police immediately deployed their dogs, hoping to catch Asha's scent and trace her steps. However, the dogs were unsuccessful, adding to the growing sense of unease.

Iquilla Degree, gripped by a mother's instinct and desperation, took to the streets. Her voice, calling out for Asha, broke the morning stillness, reverberating through the neighborhood. By 7 a.m., her calls had roused the entire community from their slumber. The Degrees' plight touched the hearts of friends, family, and neighbors alike. People canceled their plans for the day, rallying together to assist the police in a thorough search of the vicinity. The local church, a cornerstone of the community and a source of solace for the Degrees, played a crucial role. The pastor, along with other area clergymen, arrived at the Degrees' home, offering spiritual support and strength in this harrowing time.

As the day wore on, the search intensified, but yielded little. A mitten was found, but it brought no hope; Iquilla confirmed it wasn't Asha's, noting that none of her winter clothing was missing. This clue, albeit small, was disheartening. Meanwhile, the local news coverage of Asha's disappearance prompted the two drivers who had seen her in the early hours of the morning to come forward. Their accounts added a crucial piece to the puzzle, describing Asha walking along the road and her sudden flight into the woods when approached.

The following day, February 15, brought a glimmer of hope. In a shed at a nearby business along the highway, close to where Asha was last seen, candy wrappers were discovered. Accompanying these were items that tugged at the heartstrings - a pencil, a green marker, and a yellow hairbow, all belonging to Asha. Among these personal items was also a photograph of an unidentified Black girl, approximately Asha's age. This photograph, intriguing and yet mysterious, became the sole trace of Asha found during the initial search.

On February 16, a new revelation emerged. Iquilla noticed that some of Asha's favorite clothing, including a distinctive pair of blue jeans with a red stripe, was missing from her bedroom. This discovery added another layer to the mystery, suggesting Asha had perhaps planned her departure.

Despite the community's valiant efforts, the extensive search was eventually called off a week later. A staggering 9,000 man-hours had been dedicated to scouring a 2-3-mile radius around the last known sighting of Asha. Flyers peppered the area, and over 300 leads, ranging from possible sightings to tips about abandoned structures, were pursued. Yet, as County Sheriff Dan Crawford lamented during a press conference, they were still without that crucial, substantial lead. His plea to the media to keep Asha's story alive was not just a request for assistance; it was a call to keep hope burning in a case shrouded in mystery and despair.

On February 22, 2000, during a pivotal news conference, Sheriff Dan Crawford unveiled a significant shift in the search strategy for Asha Degree. Emphasizing a "long-range" approach, he announced the involvement of major investigative bodies: the Federal Bureau of Investigation (FBI) and North Carolina's State Bureau of Investigation (SBI). Both agencies promptly included Asha in their databases of missing children, expanding the search's reach and resources. While the immediate vicinity of Asha's home and her last known route had been thoroughly combed, Crawford assured the public that every lead and possibility was being actively pursued.

Investigators, drawing on Iquilla Degree's recounting of what Asha had taken with her, surmised that her departure was premeditated, unfolding over several days prior to her disappearance. SBI agent Bart Burpeau highlighted the unusual nature of the case, pointing out that Asha didn't fit the profile of a typical runaway, given her young age and lack of apparent issues at home or school. An FBI agent concurred, noting the absence of factors commonly associated with runaway children, such as family discord or academic struggles. Nevertheless, the prevailing theory among investigators was that Asha had initially run away, but may have subsequently lost her way or encountered foul play.

The disappearance of Asha Degree swiftly captured national media attention. In a bid to amplify awareness, the Degree family appeared on "The Montel Williams Show" a month after Asha's disappearance. The story also found its way onto other major platforms, including segments on "America's Most Wanted" and "The Oprah Winfrey Show," casting a wider net in the search for Asha.

March 2000 saw a further push to keep Asha's case in the public eye. Police installed a full-size, color billboard along Highway 18, near where Asha was last seen. The billboard, featuring Asha's image and pertinent details, served as a constant reminder of the ongoing search.

In May 2001, stock car racing driver Travis Kittleson lent his support in a unique way. During an event in Concord, North Carolina, broadcast live on TNN, Kittleson featured an image of Asha on the hood of his car. He expressed hope that this exposure could aid in bringing Asha home.

A significant development occurred on August 3, 2001. During a construction project off Highway 18 in Burke County, near Morganton, about 26 miles north of Shelby, Asha's bookbag and other items were discovered. Wrapped in a plastic bag, the bookbag bore Asha's name and phone number. The FBI transported it to their laboratory in Quantico, Virginia, for forensic analysis. Though the results of this analysis have not been disclosed publicly, this discovery remains the most recent piece of evidence in the case. On the 20th anniversary of Asha's disappearance, the FBI disclosed that the bookbag contained a copy of Dr. Seuss's "McElligot's Pool" and a New Kids on the Block T-shirt, items not previously owned by Asha.

Despite these efforts, subsequent leads have unfortunately led to dead ends. In 2004, acting on a tip from a county jail inmate, the sheriff's office excavated an intersection in Lawndale. The bones found during this search, initially stirring hope, were ultimately identified as animal remains.

The ongoing efforts to find Asha Degree continued with renewed vigor and creativity in 2005. Two North Carolina companies, Servpro, specializing in water cleanup and restoration, and Republic GDS, a waste pick-up service, embarked on a unique initiative. They featured Asha's image prominently on their work vehicles, transforming them into moving billboards raising awareness for her case. Republic GDS's area president, Drew Isenhour, expressed the company's singular mission in this endeavor: to find Asha Degree and, by doing so, pave the way for aiding other missing children. For a period of 30 to 60 days, 28 vehicles bore an age-progressed photo of Asha, created by the FBI, giving the public a glimpse of how she might look at a more advanced age.

The Degrees themselves were unwavering in their efforts to keep their daughter's memory and case at the forefront of public consciousness. In 2008, they initiated a scholarship in Asha's name, offering support to a deserving local student, thereby transforming their personal tragedy into an opportunity for others. Additionally, they organized an annual walk, not just a mere memorial, but a proactive event to raise awareness and funds for the ongoing search. Starting from their home and culminating at Asha's missing person's billboard on Highway 18, the walk symbolized a journey of hope and remembrance. Initially held on February 14, the date was shifted to early February in subsequent years, as Harold and Iquilla sought to balance the solemnity of the occasion with the celebratory spirit of Valentine's Day.

Iquilla Degree poignantly addressed an uncomfortable truth in a 2013 interview with Jet. She reflected on the disparity in media attention given to missing children's cases, highlighting that Asha's disappearance, as a Black child, did not receive the same level of coverage as similar cases involving white children. Her candid observation pointed to an underlying issue of racial bias in media reporting.

The case took a significant turn in February 2015 when the FBI, together with local law enforcement agencies, announced a renewed examination of the case. This resurgence of effort included re-interviewing witnesses and a substantial reward offer of up to $45,000 for information leading to the resolution of Asha's disappearance. In May 2016, this reinvestigation yielded a potentially crucial lead: Asha may have been seen getting into a distinctive dark green 1970s Lincoln Continental Mark IV, or possibly a Ford Thunderbird, exhibiting rust around its wheel wells, near where she was last seen.

September 2017 marked the arrival of the FBI's Child Abduction Rapid Deployment (CARD) team in Cleveland County, bringing an arsenal of investigative, technical, and analytical expertise to the case. For ten days, they worked intensively alongside local agents, conducting approximately 300 interviews and regularly convening with local agencies to review ongoing developments in the investigation.

In October 2018, the focus shifted to specific items found in Asha's bookbag: "McElligot's Pool" by Dr. Seuss, borrowed from the Fallston Elementary School library, and a New Kids on the Block concert T-shirt. Investigators emphasized the significance of these items as potential clues leading to Asha's whereabouts.

In a surprising turn of events, in November 2020, Marcus Mellon, an inmate convicted of sex crimes against children, penned a letter to The Shelby Star claiming knowledge of Asha's fate. However, by February 2021, Cleveland County Sheriff Alan Norman announced that Mellon's claims had unfortunately led to yet another dead end in the quest to uncover the truth about Asha Degree's disappearance. The relentless pursuit of answers continues, fueled by the hope that one day, the mystery surrounding Asha's fate will be resolved.

Brandon Lawson

Brandon Mason Lawson's story begins in the vibrant city of Fort Worth, Texas, where he was born on November 18, 1986, to his loving parents, Brad and Kimberly Lawson. Growing up in a bustling household, he shared his childhood with his sister Brittany and two brothers, Kyle and Billy, creating a tapestry of memories filled with familial warmth and bonding.

As a teenager, Brandon's life took a romantic turn when he met Ladessa Lofton at his high school. The spark between them was undeniable, and their relationship blossomed into a deep, enduring partnership. Together, they welcomed the joy of parenthood, raising three beautiful children in a home filled with love and laughter.

Brandon was the epitome of a hardworking individual, a trait that shone brightly in his professional life. He dedicated countless hours each week working in the oil fields for Renegade Well Services, a testament to his strong work ethic and commitment to providing for his family. His passion for the outdoors was another defining aspect of his life. Brandon found solace and joy in nature, often spending his free time fishing and camping, activities that he cherished deeply.

A devoted father, Brandon's world revolved around his children. He shared his love for the outdoors with them, teaching them the value of nature and the importance of hard work and perseverance. His dedication to his family was unwavering, and he was always ready to go the extra mile to ensure their happiness and well-being.

However, Brandon's life was not without its challenges. He struggled with substance abuse, a battle that he fought with determination and resilience. His journey towards sobriety was a testament to his strength of character. At the time of his disappearance, Brandon had achieved a significant milestone, having been clean for approximately six months. This period marked a hopeful chapter in his life, as he was also on the cusp of beginning a new job, a change that promised new beginnings and opportunities.

On the fateful evening of August 8th, 2013, in the quiet town of San Angelo, Texas, a seemingly routine day turned into a pivotal moment in the lives of 26-year-old Brandon Lawson and his common-law wife, Ladessa. The couple, who had built a life together over 10 years, found themselves embroiled in a heated argument, the kind that tests the strength and resilience of any relationship.

The conflict that night was not just a sudden outburst but the culmination of mounting pressures and unspoken fears. Brandon, who had been tirelessly working over 60 hours a week, was grappling with the demands of his job and the responsibilities of being a father to three young children. These stressors had cast a shadow over their household, creating an environment ripe for misunderstandings and tensions.

Compounding these challenges was a deep-seated worry that had taken root in Ladessa's mind. The previous night, Brandon hadn't come home, stirring fears that he might be slipping back into old habits of substance abuse. This concern was not just about his well-being but also about the stability and future of their family.

In their relationship, Brandon and Ladessa had established a rule to navigate such turbulent times. Whenever disagreements escalated, they would physically separate themselves - retreating to different rooms or one leaving the house - to allow tempers to cool and to approach the situation with clearer minds later. But that night, the usual protocol seemed insufficient to bridge the growing divide.

Seeking solace and guidance, Brandon reached out to his father, Brad Lawson, around 11:30 p.m. In a conversation filled with emotion and urgency, he confided in his father about the argument and expressed a desire to drive over to his house in Crowley, Texas, which was a three-hour journey away. Brad, sensing the stress and fatigue in his son's voice, tried to dissuade him from undertaking the long drive late at night. Yet, Brandon was adamant.

In the days that followed, Ladessa was haunted by a profound sense of regret and what-ifs. She lamented over the harsh words exchanged and the irreversible course of events that unfolded. "For a long time I blamed myself," she reflected with a heavy heart, burdened by the realization that their last conversation would linger as a painful memory.

"I will never get those words back," Ladessa mourned, her words echoing the deep sorrow of losing not just a partner but a decade-long companion in life.

It was 11:54 p.m. when Brandon Lawson, in a state of turmoil, left his home in his silver Ford F-150, a departure shrouded in mystery and foreboding. Little did anyone know that this exit marked not just the end of an argument but the beginning of an enduring and perplexing mystery, as Brandon Lawson would never return home.

The drive to Crowley, intended as a refuge from the turmoil back home, was abruptly interrupted when Brandon's truck ran out of gas. Stranded on Route 277, a desolate stretch between San Angelo and Bronte in Coke County, Texas, Brandon found himself in a predicament that would soon spiral into a perplexing mystery.

In need of assistance, Brandon reached out to his brother Kyle, who lived a mere mile away from Brandon and Ladessa's home. In a tone mixed with urgency and distress, Brandon requested Kyle to bring him gas. During this conversation, Brandon divulged a startling claim — he was being pursued by three men, whom he described as "Mexicans in the neighborhood." This revelation, while alarming, also raised doubts in Kyle's mind. Concerned for his brother's well-being, Kyle questioned if Brandon was under the influence of drugs and perhaps hallucinating. However, Brandon firmly denied this.

Kyle, trying to piece together the situation, contacted Ladessa to inform her about the unfolding events. In response, Ladessa prepared a fuel container for Kyle to pick up, all the while readying herself for bed, unaware of the gravity of the situation that was about to unfold.

Accompanied by his wife Audrey and their four-year-old child, Kyle went to retrieve the fuel container. Financial constraints at the time meant Kyle couldn't afford to fill it up. Thus, the plan was to collect Brandon, drive him to a service station, and have him pay to fill the canister.

Upon reaching the designated location, they were met with an eerie scene. Brandon's truck was parked haphazardly on the side of the road, its presence an ominous marker in the dead of night. But Brandon himself was conspicuously absent.

The situation escalated when a sheriff's deputy arrived shortly after, summoned by a trucker who had reported Brandon's vehicle as a hazard, dangerously positioned over the white line at the edge of the highway.

In a phone call that only deepened the mystery, Brandon cryptically told Kyle, "I can see you. I'm right here." Yet, perplexingly, neither Kyle nor the deputy could spot him.

As the minutes ticked by with no sign of Brandon, Kyle entertained the thought that his brother might be evading the officer due to a recently discovered outstanding warrant from 2005 in Johnson County related to drug charges.

But this theory, like many others, would be cast into doubt by the haunting contents of Brandon's later 911 call, hinting at a scenario far more complex and alarming than initially perceived. The call, a desperate plea for help, suggested that Brandon's disappearance was not a mere act of evasion but something much more sinister and inexplicable.

The night Brandon Lawson disappeared was marked by a bewildering series of phone calls, each adding to the tapestry of an unsolved mystery. The saga began at 11:30 p.m., when Brandon reached out to his father, Brad, setting in motion a series of events that would lead to his puzzling vanishing. Nearly half an hour later, at 11:54 p.m., he left his home, heading toward his father's residence.

The situation took a dramatic turn at 12:30 a.m. when Brandon, stranded and desperate, called his brother Kyle to inform him that he had run out of gas on Route 277 and was being pursued by unknown individuals. This alarming claim was soon followed by an even more distressing development. At 12:50 a.m., Brandon made an urgent call to 911, a conversation that would later become a critical piece of the investigation, shrouded in ambiguity and urgency.

In a rapid sequence, at 12:51 a.m., Kyle tried to connect with Brandon, leaving a voicemail, and simultaneously, Brandon attempted to reach Ladessa, only to find her phone unreachable in her car. A minute later, at 12:52 a.m., Brandon called Audrey, Kyle's wife, uttering the haunting words, "Audrey, Audrey, I'm bleeding," which would be his last known spoken words.

The following minutes saw a flurry of attempted communications. Kyle called Brandon at 12:54 a.m., followed by Brandon reaching out to a neighbor at 12:57 a.m., and then a series of back-and-forth calls between Brandon and

Kyle at 12:58 and 12:59 a.m. At 1:04 a.m., a 911 dispatcher tried to reconnect with Brandon to glean more information about his precarious situation, but only a voicemail could be left.

The night's communication culminated with Brandon making three calls to Kyle at 1:09 a.m., and two final calls at 1:15 a.m., the last instances his phone would be used. By 1:19 a.m., an eerie silence had fallen. All subsequent calls to Brandon's phone were met with an abrupt transfer to voicemail, signaling an abrupt end to the night's frantic exchanges and the beginning of a lasting mystery that continues to perplex and haunt those involved.

The enigmatic 911 call made by Brandon Lawson on the night of his disappearance has been the subject of intense scrutiny and debate over the years. The call, mired in ambiguity and distorted by poor reception, offers a cryptic glimpse into the perilous situation Brandon found himself in. Piecing together the words and sounds from this call has led to numerous interpretations, each adding layers of complexity to the already baffling case.

In one widely discussed transcript of the call, Brandon's sense of urgency and fear is palpable. The operator's attempts to clarify his situation are met with disjointed responses from Brandon, painting a picture of chaos and confusion. Brandon mentions being in a field, running out of gas near Abilene on the Bronte side, and being pursued by someone. His words suggest a confrontation: "I tried talking to 'em. I totally ran into them... Just the first guy." The call is interspersed with inexplicable noises, and at one point, Brandon chillingly claims, "I got shot," before requesting the police rather than an ambulance.

The nature of the background noises in the call has been a point of significant speculation. Some listeners have interpreted these sounds as gunshots, while others suggest they might have been the mundane noises of vehicles crossing a nearby bridge. The inability to definitively identify these sounds adds a layer of mystery to the call.

Further adding to the enigma is the operator's attempt to reach Brandon again, which went unanswered, leading to a voicemail. This unanswered return call is particularly puzzling given that Brandon made several calls after the 911 call. The reason for his lack of response remains a matter of conjecture, with poor cell reception being a likely culprit.

Compounding the mystery, some analysts of the call believe they can hear a third voice in the background. In slowed-down versions of the call, there are claims of faint, indistinct utterances that sound like "Get up" and "Protect yourself," suggesting the possible presence of another individual or individuals during the call.

As the hours stretched into morning following his last contact, Brandon's family, engulfed in worry and confusion, continued their exhaustive search for him, combing through the landscape with a growing sense of urgency. But their efforts were met with silence; Brandon seemed to have vanished as if swallowed by the night itself.

Initially, law enforcement entertained the theory that Brandon might be evading capture due to an outstanding warrant. This idea, however, seemed increasingly implausible given the desperate tone of his 911 call, where he specifically requested police assistance. This contradiction only deepened the mystery surrounding his disappearance.

Determined to uncover the truth, Ladessa, along with other family members, spearheaded another extensive search operation. They scoured the area tirelessly, facing obstacles along the way, including local landowners who denied them access to their properties, severely limiting the scope of their search. In a significant move, Ladessa even financed an aerial search, enlisting the help of a plane in the hope of covering more ground and uncovering any clue that might lead to Brandon. Despite these valiant efforts, they found not a single piece of evidence to shed light on Brandon's fate.

In the days following, deputies conducted their own search, albeit on a smaller scale. They traversed the area, looking for any sign of Brandon, but their search yielded neither a body nor any indication of human presence. Tom Green County Sheriff Nick Hanna, the Texas Ranger and lead investigator at the time, speculated that Brandon's remains might lie hidden in the desolate and treacherous desert terrain off U.S. 277, a region dominated by rattlesnakes and feral hogs.

Sheriff Hanna marshaled a significant search operation in the Bronte area. This effort included two Department of Public Safety helicopters, all-terrain vehicles, Texas Search and Rescue (TEXSAR) personnel, six cadaver dogs, and members from four different agencies. Yet, despite this formidable search ensemble, Brandon remained elusive, leaving no trace in the rugged landscape.

One intriguing piece of information emerged from a report stating that the only sign of human presence was a spot under a tree, close to the roadway and within sight of where Brandon's pickup had broken down. It appeared as though someone had sat there, but this clue, isolated and enigmatic, offered little in the way of answers.

One prevalent idea is the possibility of a drug-induced hallucination. This theory emerged after Kyle, Brandon's brother, revealed that Brandon had relapsed into using methamphetamine shortly before his disappearance. This fact led many to speculate that he might have been hallucinating on the night he vanished, potentially leading to a tragic misadventure in the harsh Texas terrain or an unfortunate encounter with the region's wild hogs.

Another grim theory suggests that Brandon may have fallen victim to foul play, possibly murdered for being in the wrong place at the wrong time. This theory is partly based on the unsettling sounds that resemble gunshots and the unidentified voices heard in the background of his 911 call, coupled with Brandon's own claims of being pursued. Supporters of this theory believe that

Brandon might have unwittingly witnessed something he wasn't supposed to see and was subsequently silenced.

Early in the investigation, there was also speculation by law enforcement that Brandon might have chosen to disappear voluntarily, perhaps to evade his outstanding arrest warrant. This theory seemed to gain some traction when it was discovered that Brandon had cashed in his 401(k) just before he went missing. However, Ladessa, Brandon's partner, strongly disputed this theory, emphasizing that Brandon cherished his children too much to leave them and that the arrest warrant was not a significant issue, as they were actively working to resolve it legally. Additionally, there has been no activity on Brandon's bank accounts or Social Security Number since he vanished, casting doubt on this theory.

Brandon's father, Brad Lawson, also expressed skepticism about the theory that his son left voluntarily. However, he harbored doubts about Brandon dying near the field where he was last seen, citing the lack of physical evidence in the rugged, cactus-strewn terrain. He held onto hope, believing that the absence of concrete evidence of Brandon's demise meant there was still a chance of finding him.

Adding to the mystery is the detail that Brandon's phone's last signal, at 1:19 a.m., was located three miles from his abandoned truck. This has led some to wonder whether he might have been picked up by a passerby, further complicating the circumstances of his disappearance.

The saga took a significant turn on February 4th, 2022. On this day, a new chapter unfolded when Brandon's family announced a potentially pivotal discovery. A search party, intimately connected with the family and led by advocate Jason Watts, braved the cold and embarked on a mission near Brandon's last known location. Their perseverance paid off in an eerie revelation: they found items believed to be Brandon's clothing, specifically his shoes and shorts. This discovery, laden with both hope and sorrow, marked a profound moment in the long search for answers.

Fuelled by this finding, the Texas Rangers initiated their own thorough search of the area. Their efforts soon led to another grim discovery: human remains. While DNA results were still pending, the discovery of these remains stirred a potent mix of emotions among Brandon's loved ones. The likelihood that these remains belonged to Brandon brought them a step closer to unravelling the mystery of what transpired on that enigmatic August night years ago.

Ladessa, Brandon's partner, spoke about this development with a mixture of hope and heartache. "We feel in our hearts it's him. We feel like, who else could it be?" she told Oxygen. Her words echoed the sentiment of a family grappling with the prospect of closure after years of uncertainty. In her eyes, Brandon was not the kind of person to willingly leave his family behind, further intensifying the belief that these remains could provide the answers they had long sought.

However, the quest for closure encountered yet another obstacle. In an update in June 2023, it was revealed that the process of identifying the remains had been fraught with challenges. The advanced state of decomposition had severely limited the potential for DNA analysis, leaving the investigators with minimal material to work with. Two different laboratories had attempted to extract sufficient DNA for testing but to no avail. Faced with these difficulties, the Texas Rangers were exploring other avenues to identify the remains conclusively.

This turn of events in the Brandon Lawson case has been a journey filled with twists and turns, each step fraught with emotional and investigative complexities. As the Texas Rangers continue to pursue other options in their quest to identify the remains, Brandon's family, friends, and a community of supporters remain hopeful. The hope is that this new evidence will finally shed light on the circumstances of Brandon's disappearance and offer a sense of closure to all those who have been touched by this enduring mystery.

Brianna Maitland

Brianna Maitland's life in Vermont was shaped by the rural charm and close-knit communities of the area. Born on October 8, 1986, in Burlington, to parents Bruce and Kellie Maitland (née Fisher), she spent her childhood on the family's farm in East Franklin. This picturesque setting, near the tranquil Canadian border, was where Brianna and her older brother grew up, surrounded by the natural beauty of Vermont.

Brianna's early years were marked by an adventurous spirit and a keen interest in martial arts. She received extensive training in jiu-jitsu, a discipline that undoubtedly instilled in her a sense of discipline and strength. Her educational journey began at Missisquoi Valley Union High School, but in search of new experiences and environments, she transferred to Enosburg Falls High School in nearby Enosburg Falls during her sophomore year.

As Brianna approached her 17th birthday in October 2003, a yearning for independence and a desire to carve her own path in life grew stronger. Her mother, Kellie, recalled that there were no significant issues at home, but Brianna was drawn to the idea of living away from the farm, closer to a group of friends who lived 15 miles away and attended a different high school. This pivotal decision led her to enroll in the same high school as her friends. However, Brianna's living situation became somewhat transient, as she moved between the homes of various friends. Her pursuit of independence culminated in her decision to drop out of high school by the end of February 2004. Seeking to continue her education, she enrolled in a GED program and moved in with a childhood friend, Jillian Stout, in Sheldon, Vermont, which was roughly 20 miles west of Montgomery.

In the weeks leading up to her disappearance, Brianna experienced a troubling incident. At a party, she was physically attacked by a former friend, Keallie Lacross. The reasons behind this attack were murky, though her father, Bruce, speculated that it might have been driven by jealousy related to Brianna's interactions with a male peer at the party. Despite her martial arts background, Brianna chose not to engage in the fight. While seated in a truck, she was repeatedly struck in the face by Lacross, resulting in a broken nose and concussion. Brianna took the step of filing charges against Lacross, but these were dropped three weeks after her mysterious disappearance. The police later cleared Lacross of any involvement in Brianna's disappearance, leaving more questions than answers in this unsettling chapter of her life.

March 19, 2004, was a day of triumph and mystery in the life of Brianna Maitland. That Friday morning marked a significant milestone for her - taking the GED exam, a crucial step towards her educational goals. The atmosphere was buoyant, as she and her mother, Kellie, celebrated this achievement with a lunch outing. Her father, Bruce, was away in New York for work, but the success of the day was palpable even in his absence. Kellie remembered Brianna being in exceptionally high spirits, even discussing future aspirations like college, which painted a picture of hope and ambition.

The celebratory mood extended into the afternoon as the mother-daughter duo engaged in a leisurely spree of shopping and errands. However, a subtle but pivotal moment occurred while they were queuing at the checkout line of a store. Kellie recalled something outside capturing Brianna's attention. With a brief word to her mother, she stepped out of the store. When Kellie finished her shopping and reunited with Brianna in the parking lot, she observed a stark transformation in her daughter's demeanor. Brianna, who had been vibrant and cheerful earlier, now appeared visibly shaken and agitated. Despite her concern, Kellie respected her daughter's privacy and did not probe into what had transpired. She drove Brianna to Stout's home, where she was staying, between 3:30 and 4:00 pm. Unbeknownst to Kellie, this would be the last time she would see her daughter.

Before leaving for her evening shift at the Black Lantern Inn, a well-known restaurant in Montgomery, Brianna penned a note for Stout, indicating her intention to return after work. She then set off in a 1985 Oldsmobile sedan, registered in her mother's name. The evening at the Black Lantern Inn passed without incident, and Brianna completed her shift. She clocked out at approximately 11:20 p.m., mentioning to her co-workers her need to get home for some much-needed rest, especially since she had another job to attend to in St. Albans the next day. Witnesses confirmed that Brianna was alone in her vehicle as she departed.

On a quiet afternoon of March 20, 2004, a seemingly routine call led a Vermont State Police trooper to a scene that would soon unravel into a deeply perplexing mystery. The destination was an eerie, abandoned house on Route 118 in Richford, known among locals as "the old Dutchburn house," situated about a mile from the Black Lantern Inn. It was there, backed into the side of this dilapidated structure, that Brianna Maitland's Oldsmobile was found, presenting a bizarre and unsettling tableau. The car's rear end had forcefully pierced the home's siding, and a piece of plywood, once boarding up a window, now lay atop the vehicle's trunk. Inside the car, two of Maitland's paychecks sat on the front seat, untouched. Scattered outside were loose change, a water bottle, and an unsmoked cigarette, suggesting a hasty or disrupted departure. The trooper, perhaps assuming the simplest explanation, speculated the car had been abandoned by a drunk driver and arranged for its removal to a local garage.

The true gravity of the situation, however, remained obscured for several days. Brianna Maitland was not immediately reported missing, creating a critical delay in the investigation. Her mother, Kellie, remained in the dark about the discovery of her daughter's car for five days. Maitland had left a note for her friend Stout on March 19, indicating her plans to return after her work shift. Stout, seeing the note, spent the weekend away and only on returning home on Monday did she find the note still there, untouched. Assuming Maitland was staying with someone else, Stout didn't feel the urgency to contact Kellie until Tuesday.

By Tuesday, March 23, Kellie's concern had escalated into action. She began reaching out to friends, acquaintances, and Brianna's employers, searching for any clue of her daughter's whereabouts. None had seen or heard from Brianna. In a growing state of alarm, and still unaware that Brianna's car had been found, Kellie filed a missing person report. It wasn't until Thursday, March 25, that a pivotal moment occurred. Maitland's parents provided photographs of her to the Vermont State Police in St. Albans. A trooper presented them with a photograph of the Oldsmobile discovered at the old Dutchburn house. They immediately recognized it as their daughter's vehicle. Kellie, upon seeing the photo, felt an instinctive horror. She expressed in interviews her belief that someone else, not her daughter, must have left the car in such a chilling state.

In the wake of Brianna's reported disappearance, several individuals came forward with their observations, adding layers to the mystery. One man, driving by the Dutchburn house between 11:30 p.m. and 12:30 a.m. on March 19-20, noted that the car's headlights might have been on, but he saw no one in or around it. Another passerby, traveling between midnight and 12:30 a.m. on March 20, recalled seeing a turn signal flashing on the car. In yet another intriguing account, a former boyfriend of Brianna's, returning from a night across the Canadian border, drove past the scene around 4:00 a.m. He recognized the vehicle but saw no one nearby. The following morning, the peculiar scene caught the attention of other motorists, compelling them to stop and take photographs. Among the items they noticed next to the car were loose change, a water bottle, and what appeared to be a bracelet or necklace.

In the wake of Brianna Maitland's enigmatic disappearance, the Vermont State

Police spearheaded an investigation that initially veered towards skepticism about the involvement of foul play. They entertained the possibility that Maitland might have been a runaway, a theory that seemed plausible given the lack of immediate evidence to suggest otherwise. The area around the haunting old Dutchburn house, where her car was found in such a bizarre state, was meticulously searched. Officers and search dogs combed the vicinity, scouring the land for any trace of Brianna, but their efforts yielded nothing but silence and unanswered questions.

It wasn't until March 30, 2004, a full ten days after the car was discovered, that Maitland's vehicle was thoroughly examined by the state crime laboratory for evidence. During this period, the car had been sitting in a local garage, raising concerns about the preservation of potential clues. When the car was finally returned to the Maitland family, Bruce Maitland made a poignant observation. His daughter's personal belongings, including her ATM card, glasses, contact lens case, and migraine medication, were all left inside the car, painting a picture of an abrupt and unplanned departure.

As the investigation progressed, the initial skepticism of law enforcement began to wane. It became increasingly clear that foul play was a likely factor in Maitland's disappearance. In a twist that added to the chilling nature of the case, a 2007 flyer issued by the FBI suggested that the scene where Maitland's car was found might have been deliberately staged to resemble an accident. Brianna's parents, deeply involved in the search for their daughter, publicly speculated that she could have been abducted by multiple assailants. They pointed to her jiu-jitsu training as a reason why it would be difficult for a single person to overpower her.

In a curious coincidence, the disappearance of Maura Murray, a college student from Massachusetts, occurred just a month earlier in northwest New Hampshire. Despite the proximity of the two cases, both geographically and temporally – within 90 miles of each other – law enforcement deemed them unrelated. This ruling only added to the layers of complexity surrounding

Maitland's case.

Determined to keep their daughter's disappearance in the public eye, Maitland's family took to the internet, creating a website titled bringbrihome.org. This site, active until at least 2009, offered a reward of up to $20,000 for information leading to Brianna's whereabouts. As of a March 2017 article in the Burlington Free Press, this reward was still available, emphasizing the enduring hope of the family and the community for answers. However, by June 2017, reports surfaced that this reward was set to expire in early July, adding a sense of urgency to a mystery that had already lingered in the public consciousness for years.

Just a mere week after she vanished, the Vermont State Police received an anonymous tip that sent shockwaves through the law enforcement community. This tip alleged that Maitland was being held against her will in a house located in nearby Berkshire, Vermont, approximately 10 miles from Montgomery, the town where she was last seen. The implications were chilling, and the authorities wasted no time in acting upon this horrifying lead.

On April 15, 2004, a law enforcement operation was launched, targeting the rented house inhabited by Ramon L. Ryans and Nathaniel Charles Jackson, both notorious figures with known connections to drug-related activities in New York. As the officers descended upon the residence, they had no idea what they would uncover. Inside the house, a grim tableau awaited them. Amidst a clutter of drug paraphernalia, they stumbled upon significant quantities of cocaine and marijuana, offering a glimpse into the dark underbelly of criminal activities that surrounded Maitland's disappearance. However, amidst this disturbing find, there was no trace of Brianna Maitland. The arrest of Ryans on drug charges during the raid only deepened the intrigue surrounding the case.

As the investigation progressed, law enforcement turned their attention to

Maitland's inner circle, including her close friends. What they discovered sent shivers down their spines. It was alleged that Maitland had delved into the dangerous world of hard drugs, specifically crack cocaine, in the period leading up to her disappearance. Even more unsettling, she had connections with Ryans and Jackson, raising troubling questions about the nature of their relationship and the possibility of a sinister connection.

The case took an even darker turn in late 2004 when a jaw-dropping statement arrived, this time from an anonymous "older female." The contents of this statement were nothing short of horrifying, penned in chilling detail. It implicated both Ryans and Jackson in Maitland's disappearance and an alleged murder that sent shockwaves through the community. According to this macabre affidavit, Maitland's life had met a tragic end approximately a week after she vanished. The document painted a nightmarish picture of an escalating argument over money, with Maitland lending funds to Ryans for crack cocaine. The dispute had allegedly spiraled into violence, resulting in her murder. The statement claimed that her lifeless body had been hidden in the basement of a local woman's home, who was incarcerated at the time. In a grotesque twist, it was alleged that Maitland's body had been dismembered with a table saw and disposed of on a pig farm, adding horrifying layers to an already harrowing narrative. However, it's crucial to emphasize that law enforcement, despite the shocking nature of these claims, was unable to substantiate the allegations made in this anonymous letter, leaving the case shrouded in uncertainty.

The torment of uncertainty extended beyond the investigation to the Maitland family, who endured a harrowing series of unverified anonymous phone calls. Each call conveyed sinister messages, suggesting that Brianna was "tied to a tree in the woods" or that her lifeless body had been discarded at the bottom of a lake. These ominous calls, while lacking confirmation, deepened the anguish and uncertainty that had gripped the family and the community.

The year was 2006 when the surveillance cameras at Caesars casino in Atlantic

City, New Jersey, captured a woman who bore a striking resemblance to Maitland seated at a poker table. It was a tantalizing lead, a glimmer of hope that perhaps her whereabouts would finally be revealed. However, this woman, who bore an uncanny likeness to Brianna, remained an enigma, her identity never properly uncovered. The tantalizing glimpse into the casino's security footage only deepened the mystery, leaving investigators and the public with more questions than answers.

Fast forward to 2012, and a new chapter in the investigation unfolded. Law enforcement delved into the chilling possibility of a connection between Maitland's disappearance and the notorious serial killer, Israel Keyes. This cold-blooded murderer had left a trail of terror across multiple states, including Alaska, Oregon, Washington, Vermont, and New York, where he even owned property in Constable. The mere mention of his name sent shivers down spines. However, after a thorough investigation, the FBI ruled out any potential link between Keyes and Maitland's disappearance. Their hopes of finding answers were once again dashed, and the unsettling specter of a serial killer dissipated as Keyes tragically took his own life in Anchorage, Alaska.

The year 2016 marked the twelfth anniversary of Brianna's vanishing, and it brought with it a glimmer of hope. Investigators revealed a crucial development to a local television station. They had managed to recover DNA samples from Maitland's car, a potential breakthrough in a case plagued by mysteries. The significance of this discovery hung in the air, a ray of optimism that perhaps the puzzle pieces were finally falling into place. However, the results of the DNA tests were shrouded in secrecy, frustrating the relentless pursuit of answers.

As if to further complicate the narrative, in July 2016, the very farmhouse where Maitland's vehicle had been discovered was consumed by a devastating fire. The flames devoured the structure, leaving behind a charred reminder of a place that had once held vital clues, now lost to the ravages of time and fire. The inferno added yet another layer of uncertainty to a case already marked by twists and turns.

And then, in March 2022, a revelation rocked the investigation. Vermont State Police disclosed that they had found a match to the DNA sample recovered from Maitland's car. A tantalizing breakthrough, yet the identity of the person remained shrouded in secrecy. The veil of silence was thick, but officials did offer a tantalizing glimpse into the puzzle—they revealed that the DNA belonged to one of the 11 individuals they had previously tested in connection to Maitland's case. Furthermore, they hinted at cooperation from this person, raising hopes that the long-elusive truth might finally come to light.

The case of Brianna Maitland continued to be a haunting riddle, with each development offering a glimmer of hope and a surge of uncertainty. As the years rolled on, the search for answers persisted, driven by the unyielding determination of investigators and the enduring hope of a family and a community that refused to give up. In this ever-evolving mystery, the truth remained elusive, but the relentless pursuit of justice remained undeterred.

Leah Roberts

L eah Toby Roberts, born in the serene suburbs of Durham, North Carolina in 1976, grew up as the cherished youngest of three siblings. Her early life was marked by the tranquility of suburban living, with the hum of family life forming a constant backdrop. However, when she was just seventeen, a shadow fell over the Roberts household: her father was diagnosed with a chronic lung illness, casting a pall of worry and uncertainty over the family.

As Leah embarked on her college journey in 1995, attending North Carolina State University in the bustling city of Raleigh, the family's struggles intensified. Tragedy struck when Leah was twenty; her mother passed away suddenly from heart disease, leaving the family reeling in the wake of her loss.

In 1998, after taking a hiatus from her studies, Leah faced another life-altering challenge. A serious car accident left her with a punctured lung and a shattered femur, requiring surgeons to insert a metal rod to aid healing. Recounting the experience to her sister Kara, Leah shared a moment of profound introspection: as she saw the truck she hit, she was gripped by a certainty of death, only to emerge from the ordeal with a renewed zest for life.

Taking a break from her academic pursuits, Leah found herself at a crossroads following the tragic passing of her father in the spring of 1999, just weeks before a planned field program in Costa Rica. Despite the overwhelming grief, she chose to honor her commitments and proceeded with the program, entrusting her sister Kara with power of attorney over her bank accounts, which now held the inheritance from her late parents.

As she neared the completion of her degrees in Spanish and Anthropology, Leah made a bold decision: she dropped out of college. Her siblings, Kara and Heath, implored her to persevere for just six more months, but Leah was resolute in her desire to carve a different path. She delved into the world of music, learning to play the guitar, and embraced photography as a new passion. A small, adorable kitten she named Bea became her companion, reflecting Leah's nurturing spirit.

In this period of self-discovery, Leah frequented local coffeehouses, her mind brimming with thoughts on life's meaning, which she poured into her poetry-filled journals. It was during this time that she formed a deep bond with Jeannine Quiller and her roommate, Nicole Bennett. Inspired by the iconic Beat Generation novelist Jack Kerouac, the trio entertained dreams of a grand road trip to the West, a journey of self-discovery and liberation. Leah, amidst her personal trials and tribulations, stood at the precipice of a new chapter, her spirit undeterred, ready to embrace the unknown.

On the brisk morning of March 9, 2000, the world seemed to be waking up to the fresh possibilities of a new day. In this serene setting, Leah engaged in a heartwarming phone conversation with her sister Kara. They discussed Leah's future, weaving plans and dreams into a tapestry of hope and anticipation. While no concrete commitments were made, the call ended with a mutual understanding, a subtle promise that they would soon reunite and share in each other's lives.

Later that afternoon, as the sun began its slow descent, casting long shadows and bathing the world in a golden hue, Leah and her roommate Nicole solidified plans for a babysitting job the following day. It was a simple arrangement, reflecting Leah's new, unstructured life since leaving college.

Freed from the constraints of academia and relying on her inheritance, Leah had embraced a lifestyle marked by spontaneity and unpredictability.

Nicole left for work, the day unfolding as any other. Upon her return, she was greeted by the noticeable absence of Leah's 1993 white Jeep Cherokee. Leah's absence wasn't alarming at first; her recent pattern of coming and going at odd hours had become the norm. Nicole assumed that Leah was out embracing the unpredictability of life, perhaps chasing another spontaneous adventure or seeking solace in her solitary musings.

However, as the dawn of the next day broke and the babysitting appointment came and went, Leah's absence grew more conspicuous. The hours stretched on, and Leah remained uncharacteristically unreachable. Concerns began to bubble to the surface among friends and family who had expected to see her. Phone calls to the house, seeking Leah's whereabouts, went unanswered, amplifying the growing unease.

By March 11, Leah's absence had turned from a fleeting worry to a pressing concern. Friends and family, once hopeful for her swift return, now grappled with a gnawing anxiety. Their attempts to contact her met with silence, painting a picture far removed from Leah's usual, vibrant self.

The situation escalated on Monday, March 13. With Leah's whereabouts still a mystery and her silence unbroken, Kara, fraught with worry, took decisive action. She contacted the Durham police, reporting her sister missing. This marked a turning point, transforming Leah's disappearance from a personal concern to a matter of public urgency. The tranquility of the early March days was now overshadowed by the looming question: Where was Leah Toby Roberts?

On the chilly morning of March 14, the air in Durham seemed laden with uncertainty. Kara, along with Leah's roommate Nicole, found themselves standing at the threshold of Leah's room, a space once brimming with her vibrant presence. As they stepped inside, the room echoed with the silence of absence. They began a meticulous search, their minds a whirlwind of worry and wonder.

The room revealed its secrets slowly. Leah's wardrobe had noticeable gaps, with a significant portion of her clothes missing. This absence painted a picture of deliberate planning, suggesting Leah had prepared for an extended journey. Adding to the mystery, Bea, Leah's beloved kitten, was nowhere to be found, indicating that Leah had not embarked on this journey alone.

Amidst the quiet chaos of the room, a note surfaced, a beacon of Leah's voice in her absence. It read with a reassuring tone, "I'm not suicidal. I'm the opposite." Leah's words, infused with a sense of purpose and vitality, mentioned her admiration for Kerouac, hinting at a deeper inspiration fueling her journey. Accompanying the note was a thoughtful bundle of cash, about a month's worth of her share of the rent and expenses, subtly suggesting her intention to return. The note was adorned with an illustration of the Cheshire Cat's grin, a symbol resonating with mystery and whimsy.

Kara, still holding power of attorney over Leah's accounts, delved into her sister's financial trail. The records revealed a series of clues: Leah had withdrawn several thousand dollars on the afternoon of March 9. Subsequent uses of her debit card traced her journey - a motel room near Memphis, Tennessee, and then a trail of transactions for gas and food, painting a path westward along Interstate 40 and northward on Interstate 5 upon reaching California.

Leah's financial footprint came to an abrupt halt after a gas purchase shortly after midnight on March 13 in Brooks, Oregon. This sudden end to account activity cast a shadow of mystery over her whereabouts.

Seeking insight into Leah's motivations, Kara and Susie Smith, Leah's best friend, ventured into the coffee shops of Durham, places where Leah had recently woven her social tapestry. It was here they met Jeannine Quiller, Leah's confidante in discussions about Kerouac's work. Leah and Jeannine had been particularly captivated by Kerouac's 1958 novel "The Dharma Bums," with its vivid descriptions of Desolation Peak in the northern Cascade Mountains of Washington. The beauty of this landscape, as portrayed in the novel, had profoundly affected Leah, sparking a desire to witness its majesty firsthand.

Kara found solace in uncovering her sister's probable destination. Although Leah's accounts showed no new activity, nothing suggested any misfortune. Kara clung to the hope that Leah, like the characters in Kerouac's novels, was out there somewhere, experiencing the profound beauty of the world, on a journey of self-discovery and enlightenment.

As March 18 approached, Kara, filled with a mix of anticipation and concern, awaited a birthday call from her sister Leah, who would traditionally ring in to wish her a happy 26th birthday. However, that day unfolded in a way Kara could never have anticipated. Instead of a warm, celebratory call, she received a stark note from the Durham County sheriff's office. The message was urgent and unsettling, directing her to contact the Whatcom County sheriff's office in Bellingham, Washington. With a sense of foreboding, Kara learned that Leah's Jeep had been found earlier that day in a remote area of the forest, but Leah was nowhere to be found.

That same morning, in the serene and rugged landscape of Washington, a couple jogging along Canyon Creek Road, which meanders through the Mount Baker-Snoqualmie National Forest near the Canada–US border, made a disquieting discovery. Scattered clothing items lined the roadside, some eerily tied to trees and branches. At the bottom of a steep embankment lay Leah's severely damaged Jeep.

Investigators from the Washington State Patrol analyzed the scene, deducing from the Jeep's trajectory through the trees and the extensive damage to both the vehicle and the surrounding vegetation that it had been traveling at nearly 40 miles per hour when it veered off the road. The condition of the Jeep's interior, jumbled and chaotic, indicated a multiple rollover. Yet, paradoxically, there was no blood or signs of injury inside the vehicle, such as shatter marks on the glass or stretched seatbelts – telltale signs that would have been present had someone been inside during the crash. This raised the chilling possibility that the Jeep might have been empty at the time of the accident, hinting at either a staged event or a meticulously planned act.

Inside the wrecked vehicle, a makeshift shelter had been created, with blankets and pillows hung across the windows. Leah's personal effects – her passport, checkbook, driver's license, clothes, guitar, CDs, and other belongings – were strewn about the woods. Intriguingly, bits of cat food and a small cat carrier were also found, confirming that Leah had indeed taken her cat Bea on her journey, though the cat remained unaccounted for. Notably, valuables including $2,500 in cash and jewelry were left behind, effectively ruling out robbery as a motive for any foul play.

In response to this harrowing development, Kara and her brother Heath flew to Bellingham, determined to aid the investigation. They visited the crash site, a place marked by the chaotic aftermath of the mysterious accident. With the assistance of the local sheriff's office, they crafted flyers and embarked on a thorough campaign around town, pinning them in local businesses and engaging with owners and patrons, hoping to uncover any trace of Leah's recent activities.

Amidst Leah's scattered belongings, a poignant discovery was made – a box of mementos from her journey, including a ticket stub from a March 13 afternoon showing of "American Beauty" at the Bellis Fair mall theaters in Bellingham. This small but significant clue offered a timeline, suggesting that Leah had spent a few hours in the city after her arrival, following a five-to-six-hour drive from the gas station in Oregon where she was last seen.

In the bustling Bellis Fair shopping mall, near the theater where Leah had watched a movie, stood the mall's only sit-down restaurant. It was here that Kara and Heath hoped to find a thread leading to Leah's whereabouts. They surmised that Leah, ever the social and curious spirit, might have stopped here for a meal. The police, following this lead, discovered two men who vividly remembered Leah. They had been seated on either side of her at the restaurant's counter, engaging in conversations that spanned topics from Kerouac's literary journeys to Leah's own plans. One of these men provided a particularly intriguing detail: he recalled Leah leaving with a third individual, whom he overheard being addressed as Barry. He even offered a description for a police sketch of this mysterious man. Yet, this account stood alone; neither the other man nor any other patrons present could confirm the existence of this 'Barry.'

Meanwhile, at a police garage, the investigation into Leah's Jeep intensified. Now joined by the FBI, who were involved due to the interstate nature of Leah's travels, investigators delved into the car's secrets. Two critical pieces of evidence emerged, suggesting the possibility of a crime. Firstly, the substantial amount of money found in Leah's pants implied minimal spending in Bellingham, less than expected for someone who had supposedly spent several days in the city. More hauntingly, hidden under a floor mat, they discovered Leah's mother's engagement ring. This ring, a cherished symbol of her connection to her late mother, was known to be perpetually worn by Leah. Her friends in North Carolina emphasized its sentimental value, stating Leah would never have removed it voluntarily, unless she had faced circumstances causing her to lose touch with her very identity.

After an emotionally charged four days in Bellingham, Heath and Kara returned to North Carolina, carrying more questions than answers. The local police, operating under the theory that Leah might have been injured in the accident and wandered off, launched a comprehensive search. For two weeks in April, aided by dogs and helicopters, they scoured the potential area Leah could have traversed had she left the crash site on foot. Despite their exhaustive efforts, no trace of Leah was found.

Adding another layer to the mystery, security camera footage from the Oregon gas station where Leah had last been seen showed her alone and seemingly in good health. However, her behavior raised eyebrows; she repeatedly glanced out into the parking lot, an area beyond the camera's reach. This behavior hinted at the presence of a traveling companion, possibly the elusive 'Barry' mentioned by the man in the restaurant. Yet, if such a companion existed, investigators surmised he hadn't traveled in Leah's car.

In the days following the unsettling discovery of Leah's Jeep, a mysterious phone call added another layer to the unfolding drama. A man contacted the sheriff's office, his voice tinged with urgency. He relayed a sighting of Leah, as described by his wife, near a gas station in Everett, closer to the bustling city of Seattle. According to his account, Leah appeared disoriented, her behavior suggesting confusion and distress. But just as the conversation was gaining depth, the caller's tone shifted to one of panic. Abruptly, he ended the call, leaving his identity shrouded in mystery. Despite the abrupt termination of the call, the police deemed the tip credible, considering it potentially the last sighting of Leah.

In 2001, the case caught the attention of the Lifetime television series "Unsolved Mysteries." The episode dedicated to Leah's case sparked a flurry of new tips and alleged sightings across the United States. Viewers called in, reporting that they had seen Leah in various locations. However, despite this surge of interest, none of the leads materialized into concrete evidence.

Back in North Carolina, the relentless quest for answers led Kara to Monica Caison, a renowned figure in Wilmington known for her dedication to helping families of missing persons. Caison, having assisted in numerous cases that had grown cold over time, was a beacon of hope. She spearheaded the Community United Effort, a network of volunteers committed to keeping such cases in the public eye even after official investigations had reached dead ends.

In 2005, marking the fourth anniversary of Leah's mysterious disappearance, Caison orchestrated a poignant event. She organized a caravan that retraced Leah's journey across the country, from North Carolina to Bellingham. This event wasn't just a commemoration of Leah's case; it served to raise awareness about the plights of other missing persons, transforming into an annual tradition. Kara and Caison's efforts reached a national audience when they appeared on CNN's "Larry King Live." On the show, Kara expressed her profound gratitude towards Caison, sharing, "I really don't know how I would have made it through the past five years without her."

The passage of time often brings with it a glimmer of hope, a chance for new revelations. This was the sentiment that guided Kara's decision to request the Whatcom County sheriff's office to preserve Leah's car long after the initial investigation concluded. This foresight proved invaluable in 2006, a pivotal year in the ongoing mystery of Leah's disappearance. Detective Mark Joseph, who had initially led the investigation, handed over his extensive files to two keen, younger detectives, breathing new life into the case.

Upon reviewing the files, these detectives made a startling discovery: the car and its contents had never been thoroughly processed for forensic evidence. Seizing this opportunity, they set out to rectify this oversight. The Jeep, which had lain untouched in this regard, was about to reveal its hidden secrets.

A crucial, previously overlooked detail soon came to light. Under the Jeep's hood, a revelation awaited: a wire had been intentionally cut, a manipulation that would allow the car to accelerate without the need for someone to press the gas pedal. This chilling discovery confirmed the growing suspicion that the Jeep's crash was no accident, but a deliberate act, staged with the intent to deceive.

The detectives' thorough examination yielded further evidence. A lone fingerprint was found under the hood, and traces of male DNA were detected on an article of Leah's clothing. These findings steered the investigation in a new direction, leading them back to the intriguing account of the man at the Bellis Fair restaurant. This individual had previously claimed that Leah left the restaurant with a mysterious man she referred to as "Barry" – a man only he had seen.

Further investigation into this individual revealed intriguing details: he had a background as a mechanic and military experience, factors that raised the detectives' suspicions given the nature of the car's tampering. However, the case was complicated by the fact that he had since relocated to Canada, presenting logistical challenges in obtaining his fingerprints and DNA for comparison.

As the case garnered media attention, including a feature on Investigation Discovery in 2011, the fingerprint found under the hood was determined not to match. However, the wait for the DNA results continued, keeping a resolution tantalizingly out of reach.

Investigators remained undeterred, their resolve fortified by the new evidence. They continued to scour the area where Leah's car was found, enlisting the aid of dogs trained in detecting human remains and utilizing metal detectors in hopes of finding the metal rod from Leah's previous leg injury. Despite these exhaustive efforts, no new discoveries emerged.

The case of Leah's disappearance, shrouded in mystery and dotted with elusive clues, continues to captivate and puzzle. Investigators, fueled by the hope that each new piece of evidence brings, remain committed to unraveling this enigmatic case and bringing closure to a story that has long remained unresolved.

Sneha Anne Philip

Sneha Anne Philip's journey from Kerala, India, to the heart of New York City is a tale of ambition, love, and cultural amalgamation. Born into the lush landscapes of Kerala, she was soon uprooted by her family's decision to pursue new opportunities in upstate New York. They initially settled in the Albany area, known for its rich history and vibrant community, before relocating to the quaint hamlet of Hopewell Junction in Dutchess County, a place teeming with small-town charm and close-knit community vibes.

In 1991, Sneha's academic prowess led her to the prestigious halls of Johns Hopkins University, where she graduated with aspirations of healing and helping others. This dream steered her to the Chicago School of Medicine in 1995, marking the beginning of a pivotal chapter in her life. It was here that she met Ron Lieberman, a fellow medical student from Los Angeles. Ron, a musician at heart, and Sneha, with her passion for painting, found in each other not just romantic partners but creative soulmates. Their shared interests and dreams knitted them closer, leading Sneha to take a sabbatical. She spent a year in Italy, immersing herself in its artistic heritage, allowing the couple to align their graduation timelines.

Their journey took them next to the bustling streets of New York City. Both secured coveted internships—Lieberman at the Jacobi Medical Center in the Bronx, and Sneha at Cabrini Medical Center, conveniently close to their East Village apartment. This period was marked by long hours and the challenges of medical training, yet it was imbued with the excitement and energy of city life.

In May 2000, the couple's love culminated in a beautiful wedding in Dutchess County. The ceremony was a unique blend of Jewish and Saint Thomas Syrian Christian traditions, reflecting the rich cultural backgrounds they both came from. Ron presented Sneha with a minnu, a traditional Malayali Syrian Christian wedding pendant. This gold teardrop-shaped pendant, with a diamond set in its heart, symbolized their union and shared heritage.

Post-marriage, the couple upgraded their living situation, moving to a more spacious apartment in Battery Park City. This move not only represented a new chapter in their lives but also a step closer to their dreams in the medical field.

The mysterious disappearance of Sneha Anne Philip on September 10, 2001, unfolds like a narrative brimming with unanswered questions and poignant moments. That fateful day, a seemingly ordinary Monday, Sneha was enjoying a day off from her demanding medical career. Her husband, Ron Lieberman, recounted that Sneha had plans to tidy their apartment in preparation for a special dinner with her cousin, scheduled for two nights later. These moments of domestic normalcy contrast sharply with the enigma that would soon envelop her whereabouts.

Earlier in the day, Sneha engaged in a lengthy, two-hour online conversation with her mother. During this chat, she expressed excitement about an upcoming visit to the Windows on the World restaurants located atop the North Tower of the World Trade Center. This iconic location was set to be the venue for a friend's wedding in the spring of the following year. By 4 p.m., Sneha signed off from her chat, stepping out to run errands, including dropping clothes at a local dry cleaner and embarking on a shopping spree at Century 21. Here, she made several purchases, including lingerie, a dress, pantyhose, bed linens, and three pairs of shoes. Little did anyone know, these mundane acts would become the last confirmed sightings of Sneha. A security camera at Century 21 captured her during this shopping expedition, providing a haunting glimpse into her final known moments.

The night progressed, and Lieberman returned to their apartment after midnight, only to find it devoid of Sneha's presence. Considering her recent pattern of staying out late, Lieberman wasn't immediately alarmed. He resolved to discuss communication expectations with her, should she stay out late again. With an early morning ahead, he retired to bed, unaware of the gravity of the situation unfolding.

A perplexing clue emerged during the subsequent investigation. A call was made to Lieberman's cell phone from their apartment at 4 a.m. Lieberman, groggy and disoriented, checked his voicemail but had little recollection of the call. When he awoke at 6:30 a.m., Sneha's absence stretched into the morning light, an ominous silence hanging in the air.

The world dramatically changed on September 11, with the horrific attacks on the World Trade Center. Amidst this chaos, Lieberman, utilizing his medical credentials, managed to return to their apartment, now shrouded in dust from the collapsed towers. Inside, the only traces were the playful tracks of their two kittens, with no sign of human activity.

In the aftermath of September 11, Sneha Anne Philip became one of the many reported missing. Her family, engulfed in despair and hope, plastered the city with flyers seeking information. Unlike others who were tragically caught in the attacks, Sneha's disappearance bore no direct link to the event. In a desperate bid to garner media attention, her brother misleadingly claimed to have last heard from her during the attack. Despite these efforts, Sneha's fate remains a haunting enigma, her story etched into the tapestry of one of history's darkest days, leaving a lingering question - what happened to Sneha Anne Philip?

The quest to unravel the mystery of Sneha Anne Philip's disappearance led Ron Lieberman on a relentless pursuit, piecing together clues like a jigsaw puzzle with missing pieces. In a bid to track her last known activities, Lieberman contacted American Express. The revelation of Sneha's credit card transactions from the evening before her disappearance spurred him to distribute flyers across various Century 21 stores, a move born out of desperation and hope.

This effort bore fruit when a clerk, temporarily assigned to a Brooklyn store following the 9/11 attacks, recalled Sneha's frequent visits. On the pivotal evening of September 10, the clerk distinctly remembered Sneha accompanied by another young woman, possibly of Indian descent. This added a new layer to the mystery. However, after scrutinizing the store's videotape footage for three grueling weeks, Lieberman discovered only the haunting solo image of Sneha browsing in the coat department, with no sign of the mysterious companion.

Frustrated with the police's initial assumption that Sneha was a casualty of the September 11 attacks, Lieberman enlisted the expertise of private investigator Ken Gallant. Gallant's investigation unearthed two critical pieces of evidence. The first was a call made from the apartment to Lieberman's cell phone in the early hours of September 11. The second, a glimmer of hope, was a videotape from the building's security cameras. Timestamped at 8:43 a.m., mere minutes before the North Tower tragedy, the footage showed a woman, a silhouette against the harsh sunlight, entering the building, lingering near the elevator, and then exiting. The woman's hair and dress, barely discernible, bore striking similarities to Sneha as captured in the Century 21 footage. Although her family insisted that the woman's mannerisms mirrored Sneha's, the uncertainty remained - she carried no shopping bags from her last known excursion and was alone.

While Lieberman could not conclusively identify the woman as Sneha, an NYPD investigator believed it could be her. This faint hope, however, was tempered by the absence of any bags Sneha would have had from her shopping trip, adding to the enigma.

Gallant initially entertained the theory that Sneha might have seized the chaos of the attack to escape a life mired in personal troubles, perhaps to start anew under a different identity. But this hypothesis crumbled under scrutiny; her computer's hard drive offered no clues of such plans, and she had left behind personal essentials - glasses, passport, driver's license, and all her credit cards, except the American Express card. Lieberman kept the account active, a beacon in the dark, hoping for a lead, but it remained untouched.

As the investigation matured, Gallant and Lieberman gravitated towards a somber theory. They speculated that Sneha, driven by her physician's oath and instinct, rushed to the World Trade Center site to offer medical aid in the wake of the attack. This act of bravery, they feared, led to her untimely demise, lost either within the collapsing towers or in the catastrophic aftermath.

The investigation by the New York Police Department was hampered in its early stages due to the overwhelming aftermath of the September 11 attacks. When they finally delved into her case, the detectives uncovered a series of complex and troubling details about Sneha's life leading up to that fateful day, painting a picture that suggested she might have been in peril or even deceased before the towers collapsed.

Sneha's professional life, prior to September 11, was marred by challenges and controversies. Earlier in the year, she faced a significant setback when Cabrini Medical Center decided not to renew her contract. The reasons cited were issues related to persistent tardiness and alcohol-related incidents, effectively amounting to her dismissal. This professional blow led to a troubling incident shortly afterwards. Sneha had gone out to a bar with some colleagues from Cabrini, which unexpectedly resulted in her spending a night in jail. During this time, she lodged a complaint against a fellow intern, accusing him of groping her. However, the investigation into this accusation took a dramatic turn. The prosecutor decided to drop the sexual abuse charge and instead charged Sneha with third-degree falsely reporting an incident, a misdemeanor under New York law. Presented with an option to recant her original complaint in exchange for dropping the charge, Sneha refused, leading to her being held overnight.

Following her dismissal from Cabrini, Sneha's personal life seemed to spiral. She began frequenting gay and lesbian bars in New York City, some of which were known for their rough-and-tumble clientele. According to police reports, Sneha would sometimes leave these bars with women she met there. Adding to the complexity of her personal life, there were claims, disputed by her brother, that Sneha was discovered in a sexual encounter with his then-girlfriend. Professionally, Sneha managed to secure another internship in internal medicine at St. Vincent's Medical Center on Staten Island. However, she faced similar issues as before, including a suspension for missing a meeting with a substance abuse counselor.

On the morning of September 10, Sneha was formally arraigned on the criminal charge related to her complaint and entered a plea of not guilty. The police report detailed a heated argument between Sneha and Lieberman outside the courthouse following the arraignment. The argument reportedly revolved around Sneha's personal problems and her nocturnal outings, culminating in Sneha walking away from Lieberman, who returned home alone to prepare for work.

In a move that underscored the perplexing nature of her case, the city medical examiner, after thorough review, removed Sneha Anne Philip from the official list of 9/11 victims in January 2004.

Sneha's husband, Ron Lieberman, her brother, and other family members staunchly dispute many of the conclusions drawn by the NYPD from the documentary evidence they gathered.

Central to the family's rebuttal is the reason for Sneha's dismissal from Cabrini Medical Center. While the NYPD posited that her firing was due to issues related to alcoholism, the family presents a starkly different picture. They assert that Sneha was, in fact, a "whistleblower," who voiced concerns about racial and sexual bias within the hospital. This claim is buttressed by the hospital's later admission to a reporter that it had no records of any formal complaints made by Sneha, adding another layer of ambiguity to the circumstances of her departure.

Lieberman sheds light on Sneha's frequented visits to lesbian bars, offering an explanation that contrasts sharply with the implications of the NYPD's findings. According to him, Sneha's choice of these venues was a deliberate effort to avoid a recurrence of the unpleasant incident with her coworker. He strongly contends that Sneha's interactions with the women she met and sometimes went home with were entirely platonic. They were occasions filled with listening to music, sleeping, or engaging in artistic activities, like painting. He recalls an instance when Sneha returned home covered in paint after spending time with an artist, exemplifying the nature of these encounters.

Furthermore, Lieberman characterizes Sneha's drinking as a temporary coping mechanism to deal with the depression following her dismissal from Cabrini. He firmly believed that this phase was transient and would cease as her life returned to normalcy.

Sneha's brother also contributes to the family's narrative by outright denying the NYPD's report of him catching Sneha in a sexual encounter with his girlfriend. He goes as far as to claim that he never even conversed with the detective who documented this allegation. Similarly, Lieberman refutes the idea that the couple had a heated argument at the courthouse following Sneha's arraignment. Instead, he and the family view these police interpretations as attempts to compensate for their initial lack of attention to Sneha's case.

Steven Koecher

Steven Koecher's life journey is a remarkable tale of ambition, resilience, and exploration, beginning in 1979 in the bustling city of Amarillo, Texas. Born into the warm embrace of a loving family, Steven was the third of Rolf and Deanne Koecher's four children. His early years were marked by a blend of traditional values and adventurous pursuits. His involvement in the Boy Scouts, where he demonstrated exceptional leadership and commitment, culminated in achieving the prestigious rank of Eagle Scout.

In 1998, a milestone year, Steven graduated from Amarillo High School, setting the stage for his future endeavors. His unwavering faith as a devout Latter-day Saint propelled him towards higher education at Ricks College (now Brigham Young University–Idaho) and later at the University of Utah. There, he pursued and attained a degree in communications, a field that resonated with his innate ability to connect and engage with people. His college years were also marked by a life-changing missionary journey to Brazil, where he not only served devotedly but also mastered the Portuguese language, adding to his diverse skill set.

Post-graduation, Steven's path led him to an exciting internship in the office of the governor of Utah. This nine-month experience was a blend of learning, growth, and real-world political insight. Following this, he joined the Davis County Clipper, a bi-weekly newspaper in Bountiful, edited by his father. As a stringer, Steven's journalistic talents shone brightly, earning him accolades and awards from the Utah Press Association.

In 2007, Steven embarked on a new professional chapter with the Salt Lake Tribune's digital advertising division. His mother recalls his fondness for the job, despite the challenges of working overnight shifts and grappling with the harsh winter weather of Salt Lake City. Seeking a change, Steven relocated to St. George in pursuit of warmer climes and new opportunities.

However, the economic downturn during the Great Recession posed significant challenges. His initial role at an internet advertising firm, Matchbin, was short-lived. The job market's instability led Steven to take up a job distributing flyers for a local window-washing firm, a testament to his perseverance and adaptability. Despite these efforts, financial strains loomed, with rent arrears and looming utility cut-offs. Resolute in the face of adversity, Steven leaned on his local ward connections, actively seeking new employment opportunities and a fresh start.

On December 10, 2009, a mysterious and intriguing journey unfolded for Steven Koecher. In the early hours of the morning, he embarked on a long drive from St. George, steering his Chevrolet Cavalier through the quiet, dark roads. His destination? A 300-mile northward journey on Interstate 15 to the bustling city of Salt Lake City. There, under the city's glowing lights, he paused to refuel his car, a transaction marked by the simple swipe of his debit card.

But the road called to him again, and Steven found himself traveling further, venturing 125 miles west on Interstate 80 to the lively town of West Wendover, Nevada. There, amidst the town's unique charm, he made another stop, refueling his car once more, a routine yet crucial part of his unexpected odyssey.

Steven's journey continued, stretching another 100 miles to the serene and picturesque Ruby Valley, home to the Neff family ranch. Steven had a history with this place; it was here he had once courted Annemarie Neff and spent time in the past. Upon his arrival, unannounced and unexpected, he conveyed to Annemarie's parents his desire to see her. Although she was not there, the Neffs, ever hospitable, welcomed him and offered him lunch. As they dined, Steven shared his plans to visit family in Sacramento, California, albeit with uncertainty due to the looming bad weather. After a stay of two hours, filled with conversation and warmth, he decided to return to St. George, retracing his route with stops for gas in Salt Lake City and Springville, and a dinner break at Taco Time in Nephi. His journey home closed a loop of nearly 1,100 miles.

During this extensive drive, Steven found time to talk with his mother over the phone. They discussed his plans to join the family in Bountiful for Christmas. Despite his financial struggles, his voice carried an upbeat tone, filled with anticipation for the holiday and hope for his job prospects. He chose, however, to keep his day's travels a secret from her.

The very next day, while distributing flyers for his employer, Steven's path crossed with two young girls in a distressing situation - they were locked out of their apartment. Demonstrating his innate kindness, Steven attempted to contact their mother and, failing that, sought help within the neighborhood, ensuring the girls' safety until they could regain access to their home.

That day also saw Steven in conversation with his ward's bishop, who echoed the sentiment of Steven's positive demeanor. The bishop, aware of Steven's struggles, offered a glimmer of hope, promising a job opportunity by the start of 2010.

On December 12, Steven's restless spirit led him to the roads once again. In the morning, his phone signaled his presence near Overton, Nevada, at the northern tip of Lake Mead. By evening, he was in Mesquite, Nevada, just over the Arizona state line, where he made a simple purchase of gas and snacks at a convenience store. The purpose of this trip remained shrouded in mystery.

Three hours later, in a tender gesture of familial love, Steven was at a Kmart outside St. George, selecting a baby's bib and cookies – thoughtful Christmas gifts for his brother's family, as part of their family's cherished holiday gift exchange tradition.

The unfolding events around Steven Koecher's mysterious disappearance weave a tale of intrigue and unanswered questions. It all began with a neighbor's casual observation on the evening of December 10, 2009. They noted Koecher returning to his apartment around 10 p.m., only to leave again half an hour later. Whether he returned that night remains a lingering uncertainty, shrouded in the quiet anonymity of the late hours.

The following morning, on December 13, Greg Webb, a significant figure in Koecher's life, made a phone call that would later prove crucial in piecing together Koecher's last known movements. Webb, on his way back from Las Vegas, was concerned about making it to St. George in time for the 11 a.m. church service. He reached out to Koecher, hoping he could lead the service in his absence. Surprisingly, Koecher revealed he was also in the Las Vegas area, some 150 miles away, but offered to return if needed. Webb, not wanting to inconvenience Koecher, decided to try to make it back himself.

This conversation, and another similar call from a ward member later that morning, highlighted Koecher's unexpected location in the Las Vegas area. Yet, neither Webb nor the ward member delved into why Koecher was there, finding nothing out of the ordinary in their interactions with him.

At 11:54 a.m. that same day, a home security camera in Sun City, a retirement community in the Anthem development of southern Henderson, captured a moment that would later be scrutinized for clues. It showed Koecher's car entering a cul-de-sac on Savannah Springs Avenue. Six minutes later, a figure, believed to be Koecher, was seen walking away from the car, clad in a white shirt and slacks, and carrying what appeared to be a file folder or portfolio.

The trail of Koecher's movements continued as another camera, this time in a garage on adjacent Evening Lights Street, reflected his image as he walked north. After this sighting, Koecher vanished from view, his whereabouts becoming one of the enduring mysteries of the case.

Meanwhile, Koecher's phone remained active, a silent witness to his unseen journey. Around 5 p.m., it pinged a cell tower over 10 miles northeast of his car's location. Two hours later, it connected with another tower, this time near Henderson's Whitney Ranch subdivision. In the early hours of the next morning, the phone pinged once more, near an interchange between Interstate 515/U.S. Route 93 and Russell Road, tracing a path further north.

Despite these digital breadcrumbs, Koecher's physical presence remained elusive. His landlord's text went unanswered, and a check of his voicemail was the last known use of his phone before it presumably ran out of battery and fell silent.

The mystery deepened when, a day after the last phone ping, Sun City's homeowners' association parking enforcement noticed Koecher's abandoned car at the end of the Savannah Springs cul-de-sac. Inside, a flyer from the window-washing company in St. George offered a clue to the car's owner. Efforts to reach Koecher through the number on the flyer, and later calls to his mother, set off alarm bells. By December 17, with no one in the family having heard from him in a week and no trace of his whereabouts, Koecher was officially reported missing.

In a frantic search for answers, Koecher's brother and sister traveled from Salt Lake City to St. George, initiating a desperate search for their missing brother, a search that would captivate and puzzle all who followed the case.

The search for Steven Koecher transformed into a relentless and heart-wrenching quest for his family, taking them through a labyrinth of possibilities and locations in the Las Vegas area. Their journey was marked by visits to jails, morgues, and hospitals, each stop a beacon of hope in the shroud of uncertainty. In a particularly poignant episode, they followed a lead to an International House of Pancakes, where staff members recalled a man resembling Steven dining there consistently for three weeks. Driven by a glimmer of hope, the Koechers themselves dined at the restaurant for four consecutive nights, clinging to the possibility of a sighting. However, a detailed account from another employee about the mysterious diner's habits eventually led them to the heart-sinking conclusion that it was not Steven.

The Las Vegas Metropolitan Police Department joined the search with vigor, canvassing the neighborhood where Koecher's car was discovered. Their efforts were bolstered by volunteers, helicopters, all-terrain vehicles, and sniffer dogs, combing the area with determination and precision. As Christmas approached, the media in both Salt Lake City and Las Vegas began broadcasting Steven's story, casting a wider net in the search. In a poignant gesture, a local dairy featured Koecher's picture on their milk cartons, and the LVMPD disseminated a video on their YouTube channel, hoping to spark leads.

April 2010 saw another concerted effort to find Steven. A party of searchers ventured into the open desert south of Henderson Executive Airport, west of where Koecher's car was parked. This effort came in response to a tip relayed to a former LVMPD officer now working as a private investigator for the Koecher family. Seventy individuals scoured a half-mile stretch over two hours, unearthing bone fragments that, upon inspection, turned out to be non-human.

The Koecher family's ordeal was compounded by a tragic turn in February 2011. Rolf Koecher, Steven's father, succumbed to a brief illness, possibly toxic shock syndrome. His passing came shortly after he, alongside his wife and family, had participated in the filming of an episode of the Investigation Discovery channel's show "Disappeared," which chronicled Steven's case. The episode aired two months later, adding another layer to the family's narrative of loss and unresolved mystery.

Amidst this, a cousin of the Koechers initiated a Facebook page dedicated to Steven's case. This digital platform not only generated new tips but also sparked suggestions for further investigative approaches. Additionally, members of the WebSleuths Internet forum delved into the case, meticulously assembling a timeline based on newspaper reports and social media posts by Koecher's family and friends, piecing together the puzzle of his disappearance.

In 2015, the quest for answers continued. A local search and rescue group organized another expedition, this time scaling the hills south of Anthem. This effort was based on a different theory about what might have transpired with Koecher.

Central to the family's belief is that Steven's dire financial situation at the time might have led him to Henderson in search of a job opportunity. This theory is somewhat supported by the footage captured on December 13, showing Steven, neatly dressed, walking with a sense of purpose and direction in the suburban streets of Henderson. This image, as his brother Dallin observed in 2018, portrays a man who appeared neither confused nor dazed, suggesting he had a clear objective in mind.

However, beyond this visual snippet, the narrative of what transpired next remains shrouded in uncertainty. As the St. George police detective poignantly remarked in 2018, the knowledge about his disappearance has scarcely evolved since the moment they realized he was missing. Contrary to some theories, his family firmly believes that Steven did not voluntarily vanish to escape his challenges or to end his life. His mother recalls their last conversation on December 10, where Steven expressed optimism about finding a new job and enthusiasm about his upcoming Christmas visit home.

Further clues pointing to Steven's intention to return include the state of his car and its contents. Found in working order with half a tank of gas, the car also held Christmas presents for his brother's family, job applications, and flyers from his employer - items that underscored his plans to return to St. George. His apartment too was left undisturbed, with his personal belongings in their usual places.

Intriguingly, Steven's travel patterns in the days before his disappearance have led to speculations about potential involvement in illicit activities. However, a police dog's inspection of his car yielded no indications of drugs. Additionally, investigations into a vehicle seen in the security footage around the time Steven parked and left his car only revealed a real estate agent showing a house in the area.

Financial records and phone logs of Koecher revealed nothing out of the ordinary, except for a single automatic credit card charge to a web hosting company and an unknown phone number that was traced back to the family of the girls he had helped. Similarly, a search of his computer and internet history, along with his library borrowing records, offered no new leads. Koecher's personal diary, while documenting his financial struggles and bachelorhood, revealed no distressing problems that could explain his disappearance.

The Koecher family does not view Steven's travels as particularly unusual. His move to St. George was partly motivated by a desire to research family history in the area, often involving cemetery tours to locate ancestors' graves. His mother believes these trips were his way of keeping busy amidst underemployment.

While there's no concrete evidence pointing to murder or kidnapping, both St. George and Henderson police departments have not ruled out these possibilities. As Detective Adam Olmstead from the St. George police expressed to the Las Vegas Review-Journal, the circumstances are undeniably strange, but nothing conclusively points towards foul play.

The mysterious disappearances of Steven Koecher and Susan Powell, occurring just a week apart, ignited a whirlwind of theories and speculations, intertwining their stories in a web of intrigue and unanswered questions. Susan Powell vanished from her home in the Salt Lake City suburb of West Valley City, a case that quickly captured widespread media attention, overshadowing Koecher's disappearance to a degree. The focus on Susan's case intensified due to the swirling suspicions around her husband, Joshua Powell, and their known marital troubles. The circumstances of her disappearance were peculiar – the night after she was last seen, Joshua inexplicably took their two sons camping in Tooele County, departing after midnight. The ensuing police investigation discovered unsettling details, including two box fans drying a wet spot on the family's couch, heightening the mystery.

As the Koecher case unfolded, the internet became abuzz with conjectures linking the two disappearances. In 2010, these theories gained more traction when Joshua Powell's family publicly alleged a connection. They posited a dramatic scenario on a website dedicated to finding Susan, suggesting she had orchestrated a plot to frame her husband for murder and had eloped with Koecher. Steven Powell, Joshua's father, further elaborated on this theory in a letter to the police and FBI agents investigating Susan's case.

However, upon thorough investigation, authorities found no tangible evidence to support any link between Koecher and Susan Powell's disappearances. A friend of the Koecher family, who took over the management of the Facebook page dedicated to finding Steven, dismissed these allegations as baseless and nonsensical.

The Powell saga took a tragic turn in Washington, where Joshua Powell and his sons perished in a horrific murder-suicide in 2012. Meanwhile, Steven Powell, embroiled in legal troubles including convictions for child pornography and voyeurism – particularly following the discovery of explicit photos he had secretly taken of Susan – passed away in 2018, a year after completing his sentence. These developments, while tragic, left the question of any connection to Koecher's disappearance as an unresolved and seemingly unlikely piece of an already complex puzzle.

96

Brian Shaffer

Brian Randall Shaffer's life story begins in the humble town of Pickerington, Ohio, where he was born on February 25th, 1979. Raised in a nurturing household by his parents, Randy and Renee Shaffer, Brian grew up with a younger brother named Derek, with whom he shared many childhood adventures.

From a young age, Brian exhibited a keen intellect and a curious mind, traits that would guide his academic journey. In 2003, he celebrated a significant milestone, graduating from Ohio State University. His academic achievements were notable: a bachelor's degree in microbiology complemented by a minor in molecular genetics, showcasing his deep interest in the intricate workings of life at a microscopic level.

Those who had the pleasure of knowing Brian paint a vivid picture of a man with a multifaceted personality. He was known for his free-spirited nature, an intelligence that shone in his academic pursuits, an outgoing demeanor that made him a beloved figure in social circles, and a sense of humor that could light up any room. His jovial nature, however, was balanced by a deep-seated respect and admiration for his mother, Renee, a dedicated nurse. Her commitment to the medical field deeply inspired Brian, fueling his aspiration to make a meaningful contribution to the world of healthcare.

After his graduation, Brian took a brief detour from his educational path, choosing to gain practical experience in the medical field. He worked as a radiology tech assistant at Ohio State University Hospital, a role that allowed him to apply his knowledge in a real-world setting and further cement his passion for medicine.

However, the call to continue his education was strong, and in August 2004, Brian returned to his alma mater, enrolling in the OSU College of Medicine. His goal was clear: to become a doctor, a dream inspired by his mother and fueled by his own desire to make a difference in the lives of others. Brian's journey through medical school was a testament to his dedication and determination to achieve his lifelong ambition of joining the noble profession of medicine.

During this pivotal period in Brian Randall Shaffer's life, as he embarked on his journey through medical school, he met and began dating Alexis Waggoner, a fellow medical student. Their relationship quickly blossomed, and it wasn't long before they became a well-known and admired couple among their peers and professors. Friends, family, and acquaintances saw in them a perfect match, both passionate about medicine and deeply committed to their studies, yet finding time for the joy and companionship that their relationship brought.

Their bond grew stronger with each passing day, and it was evident to everyone around them that this was more than a fleeting romance. Within months, their relationship had matured significantly, leading their friends and respective families to speculate about an impending engagement. Among the most enthusiastic supporters of this union was Brian's mother, Renee. She adored Alexis and saw in her not just a partner for her son but a kindred spirit. Renee's encouragement for Brian to propose was a reflection of her deep affection for Alexis and her belief in their shared future.

In 2005, however, the Shaffer family faced a heart-wrenching challenge. Renee was diagnosed with myelodysplastic syndrome (MDS), a rare and serious blood cancer known for its detrimental impact on the body's ability to produce healthy blood cells, often referred to as "bone marrow failure disorder." This diagnosis was a profound shock to the family, marking the beginning of a difficult and emotional journey.

Renee's illness struck a particularly deep chord with Brian. His bond with his mother was not just built on familial love but also on mutual respect and shared aspirations in the medical field. He revered her as not only the cornerstone of their family but also as his greatest inspiration and mentor. Her battle with MDS was not just a personal tragedy for Brian but also a harsh reminder of the fragility of life, which he was studying to protect and heal.

In the midst of this challenging time, Renee decided to give her son a special gift - a trip for two to Miami, Florida, during the upcoming spring break. Brian planned to take Alexis with him, envisioning it as a much-needed respite for both of them, a chance to escape the pressures of medical school and the shadow of his mother's illness.

Tragically, the family's struggles were compounded when, on March 6th, 2006, Renee Shaffer passed away at the age of 51. Her death left an indelible mark on the family, particularly on Brian, who lost not just a beloved mother but also his guiding light.

The loss of Renee, a figure of immense love and inspiration in his life, left a gaping void that seemed insurmountable. His days and weeks were marked by a struggle to find footing in a world that suddenly felt less familiar, less welcoming.

During this period of profound grief, Brian's relationship with his girlfriend Alexis Waggoner, also a medical student, underwent its own set of trials. In a moment of despair, Brian impulsively suggested to Alexis that they run away together. It was a proposal shrouded in ambiguity – was it a serious proposition, or a fleeting thought spoken in jest? The matter was quickly brushed aside, but the underlying current of Brian's emotional turmoil was unmistakable.

A week later, in a conversation laced with pain and vulnerability, Brian told Alexis that she should consider moving on, to find happiness with someone else, as he was grappling with a profound emotional darkness. Alexis, steadfast in her commitment and love, refused to leave his side, insisting on weathering this storm together. Despite the emotional upheaval, their plans to escape to Miami for a brief respite remained intact.

The arrival of spring break, marking the end of the demanding finals, was a relief for Brian. He celebrated the occasion with his father Randy, sharing a meal that evening. Randy observed that Brian appeared exhausted, likely a result of intense study sessions, but nothing else seemed amiss. However, beneath the surface, tensions simmered within the family, particularly regarding the distribution of Renee's life insurance policy. There was a belief, though unconfirmed, that Randy perceived Brian and his brother Derek as receiving more than their fair share.

Moreover, rumors circulated that Randy intended to cut off financial support to Brian, who had been reliant on his mother's support during his college years. This rumor, while unverified, added an undercurrent of financial uncertainty to Brian's already strained emotional state.

After dinner with his father, Brian met up with his friend William "Clint" Florence. The two decided to enjoy the night, and Clint called another friend, Meredith Reed, to join them. The trio embarked on a bar-hopping adventure across Columbus, Ohio, eventually arriving at the Ugly Tuna Saloona.

In a moment of tenderness amidst the evening's revelries, Brian called Alexis around 10 p.m. He expressed his love and reaffirmed their travel plans for the upcoming Monday. However, the night took a turn when Brian and Clint engaged in an argument, the cause of which remains unclear. The disagreement ended with Brian walking away, a decision that would soon be shrouded in mystery.

As the night wore on, around 2 a.m., Clint and Meredith realized Brian's absence. Concerned, they scoured the two-story bar, including the restrooms, but found no trace of him. Calls to his phone went unanswered, leading them to speculate that he might have chosen to walk home, given the proximity of his apartment.

The next morning, Meredith drove Clint to his car, parked near Brian's apartment. Despite the lingering concern from the previous night, they did not check on Brian. Throughout the weekend, attempts to reach him by Randy and Alexis were futile.

Alarm bells rang when Brian failed to show up at the airport on Monday for their planned trip. The culmination of unanswered calls, the uncharacteristic disappearance, and the missed flight led to the inevitable conclusion that something was terribly wrong. Brian was reported missing.

The Ugly Tuna Saloona, the last place he was seen, became the epicenter of this search. Teams scoured every corner of the bar, looking for any trace that might explain Brian's sudden vanishing. But the search extended far beyond the confines of the bar. Hospitals were checked in case he had met with an accident or medical emergency. Homeless shelters were visited, entertaining the possibility that he might have sought refuge there for some unknown reason. Even dumpsters and trash cans in the vicinity were meticulously examined, a grim reminder of the seriousness and desperation of the situation. Despite these extensive efforts, not a single clue emerged that could illuminate the circumstances of his disappearance.

In a city like Columbus, known for its extensive network of security cameras – more than in any other Ohio city, including Cleveland, Toledo, and Cincinnati – the police were hopeful that surveillance footage might offer some insight into Brian's last known movements. The city's extensive surveillance infrastructure was seen as a potential ally in piecing together the puzzle of his disappearance.

Indeed, surveillance footage did capture Brian's last confirmed sighting. The footage, timestamped just before 2 a.m. on the morning of April 1st, 2006, shows him outside the Ugly Tuna Saloona. He is seen engaged in a casual conversation with two women, a seemingly innocuous interaction. After this brief exchange, Brian is observed re-entering the bar. What transpires after this moment remains shrouded in mystery.

One of the most baffling aspects of the case is the absence of any footage showing Brian leaving the bar. Despite the numerous cameras in and around the venue, there is no record of his exit. This perplexing detail has fueled much speculation and has become a focal point in the investigation.

Adding to the enigma, there was a complete lack of activity on Brian's financial fronts following his disappearance. His credit cards remained unused, and there were no movements in his bank account. This absence of financial activity indicated that wherever Brian was, he was not engaging in transactions that could offer a trail to his whereabouts.

The combination of these circumstances - the thorough yet fruitless search, the last known footage of Brian, and the absence of any financial activity - has left both authorities and loved ones grappling with more questions than answers.

Sergeant John Hurst of the local police department revealed intriguing details about the investigation. A notable point in the bar's surveillance footage caught the investigators' attention - a sudden jump cut, which sparked speculation. Could this irregularity indicate that the camera had been tampered with, potentially by a security guard or someone else with access to the surveillance system? This anomaly in the footage raised questions about whether it was an important clue in understanding Brian's mysterious exit from the bar.

Despite this curious detail, Sergeant Hurst disclosed that there was a staff member stationed at the emergency exit of the Ugly Tuna Saloona on the night Brian disappeared. This individual, upon being interviewed, confirmed that no one had used that exit that night, adding another layer of complexity to the puzzle.

The bar's proximity to a construction site offered another possible explanation. One of the doors of the bar led directly onto this site, prompting theories that Brian, perhaps in an inebriated state, might have wandered into the construction area and met with an accident. However, this theory was extensively investigated; the site was scoured by search teams and cadaver dogs, yet no evidence of Brian's presence was found.

Adding to the myriad of possibilities was the existence of a back exit from the bar, which was not covered by video surveillance. This raised the question of whether Brian could have left the bar undetected through this exit. The lack of surveillance footage of this exit meant that this theory, like many others, remained unconfirmed.

The speculations about what happened after Brian left the bar are varied and unsettling. Some believe he may have taken his own life, while others theorize that he could have been the victim of abduction, robbery, or murder. The fact that the Ugly Tuna Saloona was situated in a high-crime area only added to these concerns. The bar has since closed, but the mystery of what transpired that night remains.

Sergeant Hurst also shared an intriguing piece of information: Brian's scent was reportedly tracked to a nearby Wendy's parking lot. However, the certainty of this being Brian's scent was not absolute, leaving room for speculation about whether he was actually there that night.

Among the theories considered was the possibility that Brian chose to start a new life elsewhere. However, this theory lacked concrete evidence. Brian's girlfriend Alexis, when questioned, expressed her disbelief in this theory, finding it hard to imagine that Brian would willingly abandon his life and loved ones.

Throughout the investigation, over 100 individuals were interviewed, including the two women Brian was last seen speaking with. Yet, none of these interviews yielded any significant leads.

A point of contention in the investigation has been the behavior of Brian's friend, Clint. Initially cooperative with law enforcement, Clint later ceased communication with the police following consultation with his lawyer and refused to testify before a grand jury. His refusal to take a lie detector test, though not unusual given the unreliability of such tests, has added to the speculation surrounding his potential knowledge of the events of that night.

In the months following his vanishing, Alexis found herself dialing his cell phone every night, clinging to a sliver of hope with each call. Each attempt would end in the same way, with the call being directed to voicemail, a silent reminder of his absence.

However, three months after Brian's disappearance, something unusual happened. One night, when Alexis called Brian's phone, it didn't go to voicemail as usual. Instead, the phone rang three times. Although there was no answer, this unexpected development sparked a flurry of questions and theories. Investigators were able to trace the call; the cell phone had pinged a cell tower in Hilliard, a location approximately 14 miles from where Brian was last seen. This unexpected signal raised several questions. Had someone found Brian's phone and turned it on? Was it possible that someone had been in possession of the phone since the night Brian disappeared? These questions, much like many others in this case, remained shrouded in mystery, unanswered and perplexing.

In a tragic turn of events, Brian's father, Randy Shaffer, who had devoted himself to the search for his son, passed away on September 14th, 2008.

Randy's death was the result of a freak accident, a tree falling on him during a violent windstorm. This heartbreaking loss added another layer of sorrow to the already tragic story.

However, Randy's death brought a peculiar twist in the investigation. A message appeared on the online guest book for Randy's funeral. The message was simple yet startling:

"Dad, I love you. Love, Brian (U.S. Virgin Islands)"

This mysterious message prompted a new line of inquiry. The Columbia Division of Police took immediate action, subpoenaing the web host's records to trace the geographic origin of the comment. Their investigation led them to discover that the message was posted from a public computer in Franklin County. However, this potential lead did not culminate in any significant breakthrough in the case.

The frustrations in the investigation were not limited to the police department. Don Corbett, a private investigator hired by the Shaffer family, encountered obstacles in accessing information and evidence related to the Brian Shaffer case. His attempts to gather more data led him to file an application for a writ of mandamus, a legal maneuver to compel the police chief to release case records and evidence.

In 2020, a new glimmer of hope emerged when a photo of a homeless man in Tijuana, Mexico, who bore a striking resemblance to Brian, went viral on social media. This led to speculation that Brian might have been found. However, this hope was short-lived as the FBI conducted a facial recognition analysis and confirmed that the man in the photo was not Brian.

To this day, the case of Brian Randall Shaffer remains an open and unsolved mystery. The events leading to his disappearance, as well as his current whereabouts, continue to elude those seeking answers. The story of Brian

Shaffer is a tapestry of unanswered questions, theories, and a lingering hope for closure.

Heather Elvis

Heather Elvis, a young woman from Horry County, South Carolina, embarked on her adult life with the support and love of her family. Born to Terry and Debbie Elvis, Heather grew up as the elder sister to Morgan, sharing a close-knit family bond. After graduating from St. James High School in Murrells Inlet in 2011, Heather, embodying the independence her parents instilled in her, moved into her own apartment in Carolina Forest. Here, she shared her space with Brianna "Bri" Warrelmann, a roommate hailing from another state. Heather's life was a blend of work and aspirations; she was a familiar face as a hostess at the Tilted Kilt in Myrtle Beach and the House of Blues in North Myrtle Beach, while also nurturing her passion for cosmetology.

In the summer of 2013, Heather's life took a dramatic turn when she met Sidney Moorer, a 37-year-old married man from Socastee, who worked on kitchen equipment at the Tilted Kilt. Heather, who had expressed a preference for older men, was drawn to Sidney, and their interactions quickly escalated from casual to intimate. The budding relationship became a topic of discussion among Heather's friends and coworkers, including Warrelmann, who observed the pair's growing connection.

Sidney, while married, reciprocated Heather's affection. He would visit her at work, bringing her small tokens like coffee and bagels, and even discussed the possibility of Heather becoming a nanny for his children. This secret affair, primarily confined to September 2013, soon spiraled into a complex web of emotions and consequences. Heather's tweets from this period, filled with cryptic references to an ill-fated love, hinted at the depth of her feelings and the turmoil that followed.

The affair took a darker turn when Sidney's wife, Tammy, discovered their relationship. Enraged, Tammy forced Sidney to end the affair in a humiliating and hurtful manner, with Warrelmann recalling Sidney's cruel words to Heather. Tammy's reaction didn't stop at confrontation; she went on to send Heather explicit texts and photos of herself with Sidney, further deepening Heather's distress.

In a desperate bid to preserve her marriage with Sidney, Tammy Moorer resorted to extreme measures that bordered on the surreal. Every night, she handcuffed Sidney to their bed, a symbolic and literal manifestation of her desire to keep him close and under control. This act of restraint was complemented by her taking over his digital life; she changed his phone password to something only she knew and shadowed him relentlessly whenever he stepped outside their home. Sidney, perhaps out of love, guilt, or a mix of both, consented to these severe restrictions, hoping to salvage the fragments of their strained marriage. Additionally, Tammy's claim over Sidney was further marked by her insistence that he get a tattoo of her name above his crotch, a permanent mark of her presence in his life.

However, Tammy's obsession didn't stop at her husband. She relentlessly pursued Heather Elvis, sending her a barrage of threatening texts, some even hinting at harm towards Sidney. Heather, trying to distance herself from this tumultuous saga, responded minimally, once indicating that she was "no one you need to worry about anymore". The communication between Heather and Tammy was sparse and fraught, with Heather often receiving texts meant for Sidney, to which she would reply with minimal engagement.

Tammy's vendetta extended into Heather's professional life as well. She repeatedly called the Tilted Kilt, the restaurant where Heather worked, in an attempt to get her fired. Tammy threatened the restaurant by saying that Sidney would cease his repair services as long as Heather was employed there. This harassment affected Heather's job and well-being, as she expressed in a text lamenting the loss of work hours due to Tammy's incessant calls.

Despite these barriers, Sidney and Heather briefly reconnected via text. Sidney attempted to justify the affair, claiming that Tammy was not upset about the infidelity itself, as she too had a lover, but rather his dishonesty about it. Heather, seeking closure and peace, expressed her wish for Tammy to cease her harassment at the Tilted Kilt. Their conversation was a mix of regret, resignation, and a longing for normalcy, with Heather bearing the brunt of the emotional and professional fallout.

Amidst this chaos, Heather retweeted a darkly humorous joke by comedian Daniel Tosh on November 5, seemingly alluding to her entangled situation with the Moorers: "hey married fellas, you can either cheat on your wife OR murder her. never both. that's when you get caught." This retweet was a glimpse into Heather's state of mind, a blend of sarcasm and perhaps a coping mechanism for the overwhelming drama unfolding in her life.

The Moorers, in an attempt to escape the escalating situation, took a family vacation to Disney World on November 19, leaving South Carolina behind for a brief respite. They returned on December 11, perhaps unaware of how significantly their actions had already altered the lives of those involved, especially Heather's. The story of Heather, Sidney, and Tammy is one of passion, betrayal, and the devastating consequences of a love triangle gone awry.

As the Moorers returned to their routine life in December, Heather Elvis was on a path to healing and moving forward. Her friends and family noted a visible change in her demeanor as she tried to leave the shadows of her past affair behind. A new job opportunity at a beauty parlor in Myrtle Beach presented itself, a venture Heather was excited about, starting just before the festive season of Christmas. Alongside her roommate Brianna Warrelmann, Heather found solace and strength in spirituality, committing to attend church regularly as a means to find peace and new beginnings.

However, amidst these positive changes, Heather faced personal challenges. Her colleagues at the Tilted Kilt noticed a significant change in her physique; Heather had gained weight, and her uniform sizes had increased notably. This physical transformation sparked a deep concern in Heather – she feared that she might be pregnant, possibly with Sidney's child. The anxiety of this possibility weighed heavily on her, compounded by a failed pregnancy test that returned an "error" result, leaving her in a state of uncertainty and worry.

On the night of December 17, Heather sought to embrace new experiences and perhaps a new chapter in her life. She went on a date with Steven Schiraldi, a new acquaintance, marking her first step into the world of dating post-affair. Their date was a simple yet charming excursion, driving around to admire the festive Christmas lights in the area. The night took a playful turn when they parked at the Inlet Square Mall, where Steven introduced Heather to the art of driving a manual transmission vehicle. Heather, finding joy in this new skill, shared photos of herself with the stick shift with her father and Warrelmann, a gesture of sharing her small triumphs and happy moments.

The date concluded with Steven dropping Heather off at her apartment in Carolina Forest around 1:15 a.m., unknowingly becoming the last person to have seen her. Shortly thereafter, at around 1:35 a.m., a mysterious and pivotal event occurred – a call was made from a payphone to Heather's cell phone, lasting about five minutes. This call was followed by an emotionally charged conversation with Warrelmann. Heather revealed that Sidney had reached out to her, claiming he intended to leave his wife and wanted to meet her. Warrelmann, alarmed by Heather's hysterical state, advised her against the meeting. The call ended after two minutes, leaving a trail of unanswered questions and concerns.

From 1:45 a.m. on December 18, Heather Elvis' whereabouts became a mystery, a haunting uncertainty that clouded the lives of her loved ones and the community.

On the cold evening of December 19, a startling discovery was made that added a new layer of mystery to Heather Elvis' disappearance. Her green Dodge Intrepid was found at Peachtree Landing, a boat launch along the Waccamaw River in Socastee. This location was a significant distance, about eight miles, from her apartment. The car, oddly parked perpendicular to the designated spaces, was locked and eerily devoid of personal items like Heather's phone, keys, or purse. Attempts to call her phone led nowhere, and Heather was conspicuously absent from both her apartment and her workplaces.

This discovery prompted the Horry County police to launch a full-scale missing person investigation. Steven Schiraldi, who had been with Heather on her last known night, was quickly interviewed and cleared of any involvement. An extensive search was conducted in the surrounding area of the boat landing, but it yielded no trace of Heather. Further efforts, including a meticulous dive into the riverbed down to Winyah Bay by rescue divers from Coastal Carolina University, also turned up nothing. Adding to the tension was the discovery of a set of bones nearby around New Year's Day, which were later determined to be male, thus not related to Heather's case.

The investigation took a technological turn as detectives delved into Heather's phone records. The records revealed a flurry of activity on the morning after she had informed Warrelmann about Sidney's call. The phone's location pings painted a perplexing picture of movement and calls. At 2:30 a.m., a call was made from Heather's phone to the same payphone Sidney supposedly used earlier, followed by the phone's brief presence at Longbeard's Bar and Grill. The phone then traveled to Augusta Plantation Drive, returning to Longbeard's, and attempted to call Sidney's phone, which went unanswered. Intriguingly, the phone then appeared to be in motion, heading towards Heather's apartment, and there, another call was made to Sidney, resulting in a four-minute conversation.

The phone's final journey was to Peachtree Landing, where multiple unanswered calls were made to Sidney's phone. After that, the phone's data records ceased, its last known location being somewhere in the vast expanse of the Waccamaw National Wildlife Refuge.

The investigation then turned to scrutinizing Tammy and Sidney's phone records. Interestingly, there had been no communication between the two phones from November 2, until the early hours of December 18, when Tammy texted Sidney asking for "the pot stickers and orange juice", to which he immediately responded.

Surveillance footage became a crucial part of the investigation. Sidney was seen on camera at a Myrtle Beach Walmart, purchasing cigars and a pregnancy test at 1:12 a.m. on the night of Heather's disappearance. Further footage from a Kangaroo gas station captured Sidney making the call from the payphone to Heather's cellphone at 1:35 a.m.

The most telling evidence emerged from private security cameras along the route from the Moorers' house to Peachtree Landing. Two cameras captured a dark Ford F-150, similar to Sidney's, heading towards the landing and then returning. Although the vehicle's license plate was not visible, subsequent video analysis by the South Carolina Highway Patrol and the FBI concluded that it was indeed Sidney's truck.

On January 28, 2014, William Christopher Barrett and Garrett Ryan Starnes found themselves in police custody, charged with obstruction of justice. The reason for their arrest was the misleading and false information they had disseminated on social media about the case. This misinformation led the investigators astray, consuming valuable time and resources that could have been directed towards finding Heather. Both Barrett and Starnes were released on bond, but the charge against Starnes was dismissed in April due to a procedural oversight when the charging officer missed the preliminary hearing. The saga continued with Starnes being indicted on the charge in July.

Meanwhile, Sidney Moorer reported experiencing a series of alarming incidents, presumably as a result of the public's suspicion of his involvement in Heather's disappearance. During February, he reported to police on two separate occasions that he had been shot at or threatened with weapons while driving with his family. However, law enforcement found no evidence to corroborate his claims of gunfire hitting his truck. Sidney also claimed that he and his family were being followed, received threats against their lives and home, and that their pets had been killed and mutilated. These incidents led him to post signs outside his home, expressing distress over the threats, some of which were allegedly targeted specifically at his children.

On February 21, a significant development occurred. The police sectioned off a part of South Carolina Highway 814 near the Moorer residence to conduct a thorough search of the property. After 11 hours, the search culminated in the arrest of both Sidney and Tammy Moorer at their home. They were charged with a slew of serious offenses, including murder, kidnapping, obstruction of justice, and two counts each of indecent exposure. The indecent exposure charges stemmed from sexually explicit images found on their phones, believed to have been taken in public places. The obstruction charges against Sidney were later clarified to be linked to his initial denial of using the payphone to contact Heather, a claim he retracted only when confronted with the surveillance footage from the gas station.

The Moorers managed to post the $20,000 bond set for the obstruction and exposure charges but later waived the bond for the kidnapping charges, choosing instead to focus on the more severe murder charges, for which they were initially held without bond. In the following month, the court imposed a gag order on all parties involved in the case. Additionally, investigators announced impending charges unrelated to Heather's case, pertaining to "financial discrepancies" filed with the State of South Carolina. These charges, formally filed in June, accused the Moorers of Medicaid fraud, alleging that they had failed to report income from their businesses on a 2007 application for benefits exceeding $10,000.

Following the arrest of Sidney and Tammy Moorer, a storm of social media activity ensued, with a significant portion expressing support for the couple. Prior to their arrest, the Moorers had been active on various online platforms, particularly on Facebook, where they portrayed Heather Elvis as a stalker and suggested that the police were framing them to protect the real perpetrators. This narrative gained traction among their supporters, creating a digital battleground of accusations and counter-accusations.

The Elvis family found themselves in an uphill struggle to counter these claims. They felt overwhelmed by the scale and intensity of the online harassment. In a notable incident, they barred a local newspaper from a news conference after it had published some of the allegations against them, highlighting the tension and sensitivity surrounding the case.

In early 2015, after spending 11 months in jail, the Moorers were released following a judge's decision to accept Tammy's mother's house as collateral for the $100,000 bond set for the murder charges. During the bond hearing, the prosecution acknowledged the absence of direct evidence linking the couple to Elvis's disappearance. The Elvis family vehemently opposed the release, citing threats they had received from the Moorer family and their supporters. Consequently, the court imposed stringent conditions on the Moorers' release, including GPS monitoring, a mandate to stay at least 5 miles away from the Elvis family home, and a prohibition against interacting with any Elvis family member on social media.

The ongoing threats and the couple's struggle to find employment in Horry County led the court, in September, to permit the Moorers to relocate to Florida, where Sidney had secured a job. Despite the move, they were required to adhere to their bail conditions and agreed to waive extradition from Florida in case of any violations.

In a significant twist in March 2016, the prosecutors dropped the murder charges against Sidney and Tammy without prejudice, allowing for the possibility of reinstating the charges in the future. The indecent exposure charges and the obstruction charge against Tammy were also dropped, while the charges related to the alleged Medicaid fraud were maintained. The Elvis family, though disappointed by this development, expressed understanding of the prosecutorial decisions. They held onto hope that ongoing investigations and trials related to the remaining charges might eventually uncover the truth about their daughter's fate.

June 2016 marked a pivotal moment in the ongoing saga of Heather Elvis' disappearance, as Sidney Moorer stood trial, accused of kidnapping her. The trial, spanning four days, was a culmination of intense investigation and public speculation. The jury, tasked with a grave decision, listened intently as the state presented its case.

Witnesses, including Heather's coworkers, took the stand, painting a vivid picture of the relationship between Heather and Sidney. They testified to their belief that Heather had become pregnant as a result of their affair, a crucial point in the prosecution's narrative. Law enforcement experts meticulously laid out the phone and video evidence, drawing a line connecting Sidney to Heather on the morning of her disappearance. In a dramatic move, the jurors were taken to Peachtree Landing and the Moorer residence, giving them a firsthand view of key locations in the case.

The trial's intensity peaked on its final day with Brianna Warrelmann's testimony. As Heather's roommate and confidante, Warrelmann provided an in-depth account of the affair between Heather and Sidney. Her emotional recounting of their last conversation brought the human element of the tragedy to the forefront. The defense, in their cross-examination, probed into Heather's past, including her family issues and a previous relationship with an allegedly abusive boyfriend, attempting to cast doubt on the prosecution's narrative. Despite the defense's motion for a directed verdict of not guilty being rejected by the judge, Sidney's attorney, Kirk Truslow, rested the case without presenting a defense. In his closing argument, Truslow emphasized that the case against Sidney was circumstantial, underscoring that it only proved an affair, not kidnapping.

The jury's deliberation stretched for seven hours, culminating in a deadlock. Ten jurors were in favor of conviction, but two stood opposed, leading to an irrevocable division. This stalemate resulted in the judge declaring a mistrial. As of December 2018, a new trial date had not been set, and Sidney's successful motion for a change of venue meant that the retrial would occur in neighboring Georgetown County.

Amidst the trial, Sidney spoke to the media, breaking the court-imposed gag order. This action led to him being found in contempt of court and sentenced to five months in jail, although he was released after two months for good behavior. Upon his release, Sidney once again addressed the media, expressing his belief that the jury had not been impartial and labeling the entire case as "malicious prosecution."

In July 2017, over a year after the initial trials, the focus shifted to Tammy Moorer. A hearing was convened to decide if Tammy had breached the gag order, potentially meriting a contempt of court charge. Details of this hearing, including its outcomes and the circumstances that led to it, remained shrouded in secrecy.

Sidney Moorer's trial on the obstruction charge soon followed, marking a rare instance in South Carolina where such a charge proceeded to trial. The prosecution's strategy revolved around the crucial cell phone records and video footage from the morning of Elvis' disappearance. They aimed to demonstrate to the jury how Sidney's initial denial of making the payphone call to Elvis, which he later admitted to after being confronted with video evidence, had significantly impeded the investigation. A new twist emerged with the testimony of Tammy's cousin, who claimed Sidney had shown him something on his phone after Heather's disappearance, implying Sidney knew more than he had disclosed to the police. This claim was elaborated upon in a 2021 "Dateline" episode, where it was revealed that the cousin was referring to a disturbing photograph of Heather, appearing deceased with visible injuries.

The trial concluded after three days with Sidney's conviction. He received the maximum sentence of ten years in prison, accounting for the time he had already served. Despite the length of the sentence, it was anticipated that Sidney would be eligible for parole much earlier, though his first parole application in November 2018 was unanimously denied. As of October 2018, he was incarcerated at Lee Correctional Institution. Sidney's attorney, Truslow, announced plans to appeal the conviction. He argued the vagueness and broad scope of the obstruction charge under South Carolina's common law made it unconstitutional in this context. Truslow maintained that Sidney's deceit did not significantly derail the investigation and accused the prosecutors of seeking a conviction for the sake of closure.

In April 2018, the case took another turn when Sidney and Tammy were jointly indicted on a single count of conspiracy to kidnap. This development, the first of its kind in the case, led to speculation among legal commentators. The new charge suggested the possibility of either newfound evidence or one of the Moorers turning against the other. According to one commentator, a conviction for conspiracy would likely require testimony from a co-conspirator, indicating the prosecution might be applying pressure for one of them to collaborate.

Sidney, undeterred, continued his legal battle. In 2019, following his kidnapping conviction, he appealed the obstruction conviction. He argued that the evidence presented was insufficient and that his request for a directed verdict should have been granted. Despite his efforts, the conviction was upheld, first by an appellate court and then by the South Carolina Supreme Court.

The trial of Tammy Moorer in October 2018, almost five years after Heather Elvis' disappearance, captivated national media attention, unfolding into a dramatic courtroom saga. The prosecution's strategy involved showcasing not only the documentary evidence from Sidney's trial but also introducing Tammy's threatening text messages to Heather. These messages were portrayed as evidence of Tammy's jealousy and rage upon learning about Heather's potential pregnancy with Sidney, suggesting a motive for harm. Tammy's online behavior, notably a Facebook post where she labeled Heather a "psycho whore" and accused her of stalking her family, further painted a picture of her animosity towards Heather.

In a surprising turn, Sidney's mother testified, revealing that Tammy had physically assaulted Sidney shortly after discovering the affair. Additionally, the prosecution introduced sexually explicit texts from Tammy to another lover. The defense sought a mistrial, arguing these texts unfairly prejudiced Tammy's character, but the court denied this motion. In the same messages, Tammy had mentioned being unbothered by the affair, as she had her own extramarital relationship; it was Heather's alleged stalking that upset her. This claim was echoed in Tammy's testimony, where she claimed to have an open marriage and even described having a "nice conversation" with Heather, supposedly resolving any issues between them.

However, the prosecution's cross-examination painted a different picture. They presented evidence suggesting Sidney's affair with Heather was more serious than Tammy had admitted, including a hotel room key found in Heather's car and a receipt for the room paid by Sidney. Tammy's response to these revelations was simply to photograph the receipt with her phone. During the trial, it was also revealed that Tammy and Sidney were legally separated, partly because of Tammy's disappointment in Sidney not testifying in his defense during his trials.

The defense faced a significant setback when five key witnesses, including Tammy's children and mother, were accused of violating a court order by watching live trial coverage. Despite their denial, the judge ruled they had, barring their testimonies. As a result, the defense had to adjust its strategy, starting with testimony from Tammy's sister Ashley Caison.

Caison attempted to refute several prosecution claims. She testified that Sidney's tattoo, allegedly gotten as a mark of submission to Tammy, was actually obtained long before he met Heather. She also claimed that the handcuffs used by the couple were for sexual roleplaying, not to restrain Sidney as previously suggested. However, the prosecution challenged her credibility, citing discrepancies with her police interview.

The defense also presented Sydney Moffitt, a former roommate of Heather's, who discussed Heather's past abusive relationship and an unexplained incident where Heather had bruises. Two men acquainted with Heather also testified; one admitting to a sexual relationship with her, and the other recounting a possible sighting of Heather at a bar, which was later disproved by security footage.

During her testimony, Tammy Moorer attempted to cast doubt on the accusations against her, particularly the claim that she had handcuffed Sidney to their bed. She explained that they owned a sleigh bed, which made handcuffing physically impossible. Addressing the topic of Sidney's affair, Tammy conveyed that although initially upset, she had moved past her anger, especially after their family trip to Disneyland. On the night Heather Elvis disappeared, Tammy recounted that she and Sidney had ventured out both for an intimate encounter in his truck and to purchase a pregnancy test, as they were trying to conceive another child. She mentioned a miscarriage while in jail, and that the test result was negative. After returning home around 3:10 a.m., Tammy claimed she stayed up to attend to household chores, and that Sidney had received a call from Heather but remained at home thereafter.

In their closing arguments, the attorneys re-emphasized their key themes. The prosecutor, using a Disney analogy, likened Tammy to the Evil Queen from "Snow White and the Seven Dwarfs," painting her as a woman consumed by jealousy and capable of extreme actions. Conversely, Tammy's defense attorney highlighted the lack of concrete evidence, pointing out the implausibility of the Moorers making Heather disappear without a trace in the short time frame between Heather's last phone activity and Tammy's text message to Sidney about pot stickers.

After an 11-day trial, the jury deliberated for four hours before convicting Tammy on both charges. She received a 30-year sentence for each charge, to be served concurrently, with credit for time already served. Following the trial, Tammy announced her intention to appeal, citing the verdict's reliance on circumstantial evidence and planning to engage different attorneys for her appeal.

The day after the trial concluded, Heather's father, Terry Elvis, faced a contempt of court charge. Allegations were made by one of Tammy's attorneys, Casey Moore, that Terry had shouted insults at him in the courthouse. Terry admitted to the encounter but denied any verbal abuse, and pointed out that Moore had used the courthouse bathroom designated for the Elvis family. Despite his defense, Terry was found guilty and fined $400, which he agreed to pay despite his family's belief that the charge was unwarranted given the lengthy duration of the case.

In September 2019, Sidney Moorer was found guilty of kidnapping Heather Elvis and sentenced to 30 years in prison.

Tammy's appeal, heard in late 2021, centered on several key arguments. She claimed that the judge's decision to bar family members from testifying, due to their alleged violation of the sequestration order by following the trial live, denied her a fair trial. Additionally, she challenged the admissibility of the state expert's identification of Sidney's truck in the video, citing its subjective and unscientific nature. Finally, Tammy argued that the sexually explicit text messages between her and Sidney should have been excluded from the trial as they were irrelevant and prejudicial. The appeal highlighted the ongoing legal complexities and the emotional weight of a case that had gripped the community and the nation for years.

Danielle Imbo and Richard Petrone

Danielle Imbo, a native of South Philadelphia, Pennsylvania, was born into a family deeply rooted in the musical culture of the 1950s. Her birthdate, August 7th, 1970, marked the arrival of a soul destined to inherit a rich legacy of melodies and rhythms. Her father, John Ottobre, known professionally as "Johnny October," carved his niche in the music industry as a charismatic singer with "The Four Dates," a doo-wop ensemble that gained prominence during the vibrant era of the 1950s. This group's journey saw them evolve into a cherished backup ensemble for the renowned Frankie Avalon, a star who defined an era with his dulcet tones and magnetic stage presence.

Growing up in this melodious environment, Danielle naturally gravitated towards music. It became a vital part of her existence, an intimate friend that accompanied her through life's ups and downs. She was often seen humming tunes, her voice echoing her father's passion for music. Concerts were her sanctuaries, places where she could immerse herself in the world of harmonies and rhythms that she so dearly loved.

Apart from her musical pursuits, Danielle had a penchant for the intriguing twists and turns of murder mystery novels, a genre that captivated her imagination and offered an escape into thrilling narratives. Professionally, she carved out a career as a loan processor, demonstrating a keen mind for financial details and customer interactions.

To those who knew her, Danielle was a beacon of kindness and warmth, always ready to lend a listening ear or share a hearty laugh. Her role as a mother was her crowning achievement, and she embraced it with all her heart, dedicating herself to the wellbeing of her young son, Joe Jr., who was just 18 months old.

In a parallel thread of life, Richard Petrone Jr. was born on August 29th, 1969, in the same city of Philadelphia. The son of Richard and Margaret Petrone, he embodied the values of hard work, relaxation, and an unwavering commitment to family. Richard's life was a testament to the enduring strength of familial bonds, particularly evident in his deep connection with his 14-year-old daughter, Angela. His role as a single father was one he undertook with love, dedication, and a sense of responsibility that never wavered.

Professionally, Richard was an integral part of his family's bakery business, Viking Pastries, located in Ardmore, Pennsylvania. Here, he combined his entrepreneurial spirit with a passion for crafting delicious treats, contributing to the local community's culinary landscape.

Just like Danielle, Richard had an affinity for music, though his heart lay with the raw energy and powerful expressions found in rock music. This love for rock was a thread that connected him to the wider tapestry of artistic expressions. In addition to his musical interests, Richard was an avid sports enthusiast, with a particular fondness for the Chicago Bears. His love for sports was more than a pastime; it was a reflection of his competitive spirit and his appreciation for teamwork and resilience.

Together, Danielle and Richard shared a world where music, family, and passion intersected, creating a unique tapestry of experiences and shared interests. Their lives, intertwined through common loves and aspirations, painted a picture of two souls connected by more than just fate.

The year 2004 marked a significant turning point in Danielle Imbo's life. It was a year that began with the excitement of the Super Bowl, an event that her husband, Joe Imbo, attended in Houston, leaving behind his wife and their baby, both unwell with a cold. However, this trip turned out to be more than just a sporting excursion. Upon his return, Joe dropped a bombshell that would forever alter the course of their family's life. He had met another woman on the plane and, in a declaration that blindsided Danielle, announced his desire for a divorce. The news was a jolt to Danielle, who found herself grappling with a whirlwind of emotions: shock, betrayal, and a deep sense of hurt.

As the reality of her crumbling marriage settled in, the stress and heartache began to manifest in physical ways. Danielle, once vibrant and full of life, started chain-smoking, a coping mechanism that reflected her inner turmoil. Her health took a further hit as she lost a considerable amount of weight, a visible sign of the emotional burden she was shouldering. This period in her life was marked by a struggle to find stability and comfort amidst the chaos of a dissolving marriage.

In the midst of this personal upheaval, a figure from her past reemerged, bringing with him a glimmer of hope and familiarity. Richard Petrone, a childhood friend from the same neighborhood, reentered Danielle's life. They had grown up together, with Danielle being close to Richard's sister, but over the years, their paths had diverged. However, fate had a way of bringing them back together. Upon rekindling their acquaintance, they discovered a natural chemistry and connection that quickly blossomed into a romantic relationship.

Richard's feelings for Danielle were unlike anything he had experienced before. His daughter, Angela, vividly recalled her father's profound affection for Danielle, noting that she was the first woman he had truly fallen in love with, someone he wanted to dedicate his time and heart to. This newfound love brought a sense of joy and companionship to both Danielle and Richard.

Despite the happiness they found in each other, the shadow of Danielle's ongoing divorce loomed large. Aware of the complexities and emotional toll of the process, Danielle made a difficult but thoughtful decision. She chose to pause her relationship with Richard, believing that it was crucial to focus her energies on her young child and navigate the divorce proceedings with clarity and commitment. This decision, while painful for both, was a testament to her sense of responsibility and care for her family's wellbeing.

Richard, respecting Danielle's wishes, stepped back, allowing her the space and time she needed. This act of understanding and patience highlighted the depth of his feelings for her, demonstrating a willingness to put her needs and those of her family first.

The unraveling of Danielle Imbo's marriage to Joe took a surprising turn when, not long after their separation, Joe's new relationship came to an abrupt end. Seemingly regretful, he approached Danielle with a proposal to reunite and rebuild their marriage. Despite the lingering emotions Danielle harbored for her husband, she harbored reservations. Her marriage to Joe had been marred by issues; he was often described as controlling and prone to fits of temper, traits that made their relationship turbulent.

Their attempts at reconciliation frequently devolved into heated arguments, a reflection of the deep-seated issues between them. On one particularly distressing occasion, Joe's anger allegedly escalated to the point where he threw their son's highchair against a wall in a fit of rage, an incident he would later vehemently deny.

As these tumultuous events unfolded, Richard Petrone was experiencing a solitary evening on February 19th, 2005. Dining alone at a bar, he found himself craving the vibrancy of live music but was reluctant to go alone. He reached out to his sister, Christine, in hopes of companionship, but she declined. However, fate had a different plan, as Danielle happened to be visiting Christine at that moment. With Joe out of town and their son in his care, the stage was set for an unexpected reunion between Danielle and

Richard.

The two had not spoken for weeks, but Danielle surprised Richard by accepting his invitation. As PhillyMag profiled, Danielle, a rock band frontwoman, was known for her lively, outgoing personality. Her recent experiences with Joe had left her drawn to Richard's more gentle and understanding approach.

That evening, Richard arrived in his 2001 black Dodge Dakota to pick Danielle up, and they headed to Abilene's bar on Philadelphia's South Street. There, amidst the lively atmosphere and melodies of a live band, they joined Richard's friends, Anthony and Michelle. Observers noted that nothing seemed amiss; Richard and Danielle appeared content, sharing intimate moments and even discussing plans for the following weekend, hinting at the possibility of another date.

Despite an invitation from Anthony and Michelle to continue the night at another bar, both Richard and Danielle declined. They were mindful of their early commitments the next day and wished not to stay out late.

As the clock neared 11:45 p.m., the pair decided to leave. Richard was heard mentioning his plan to drive Danielle back to her home in Mount Laurel before returning to South Philadelphia himself. They stepped out into the night together, a couple seemingly at ease in each other's company.

However, this ordinary departure marked the beginning of an extraordinary and perplexing mystery. From that moment on, Richard and Danielle vanished without a trace, leaving behind unanswered questions and a void in the lives of those who knew and loved them.

On the morning following their night out, an unsettling silence began to set in as both Danielle and Richard became unreachable. Danielle, who was known for her punctuality and reliability, notably missed a hair appointment, an uncharacteristic lapse that raised the first red flag. As the hours ticked by, attempts to reach both her and Richard on their cellphones were met with the disquieting reality of their phones going straight to voicemail. This unusual lack of communication sent waves of concern rippling through their families.

Driven by a growing sense of unease, Danielle's brother, John Ottobre, took it upon himself to check on her. He had a spare key to her home, a symbol of the trust and closeness they shared as siblings. Upon entering her residence, John was greeted by darkness, a silent testament to her absence. A quick survey of the house revealed nothing amiss – no signs of disturbance or struggle. Yet, the normalcy of the scene did little to quell the mounting anxiety.

The alarm bells truly began to ring in the afternoon. Danielle was a dedicated mother, and her failure to return home by 3 p.m. to receive her son, Joe Jr., from his father was a glaring deviation from her routine. John, deeply troubled by this, later reflected on her commitment as a mother, stating with conviction that she would never voluntarily miss an opportunity to be with her son. "She wouldn't have missed that. No way," he would recall.

Both Danielle and Richard were known for their strong family ties and consistent communication with their loved ones. The notion of them disappearing without any form of explanation was beyond comprehension for their families.

That afternoon, when Joe arrived at Danielle's house to drop off their son, he was greeted not by Danielle but by her worried family. John, attempting to maintain a semblance of normalcy, explained that Danielle was unexpectedly unavailable and that he would take care of Joe Jr. in her stead. However, as time stretched on with no contact from Danielle or Richard, the situation escalated from concerning to alarming.

Finally conceding to their fears, the families took the decisive step of reporting Danielle and Richard as missing. This action marked the beginning of a frantic and desperate search, a search that would involve not just their families but a community and law enforcement, all united in the singular goal of finding the missing couple.

Unwilling to adhere to the conventional waiting period often suggested by law enforcement, Danielle's family, propelled by a sense of urgency, took matters into their own hands.

As darkness enveloped the city, John Ottobre, Danielle's brother, joined forces with Richard Petrone Sr., Richard's father, in a desperate quest through the streets of Philadelphia. They navigated the maze of city roads, highways connecting Philly to Mount Laurel, and every possible route that Richard's truck could have taken. Their search was methodical and exhaustive; they scrutinized every side street, back alley, and overlooked nook they came across, hoping against hope to find a clue, a sign, anything that could lead them to the missing couple.

Their search extended beyond the roads to the waterways and overpasses of the city, including major bridges like the Walt Whitman, Ben Franklin, and Betsy Ross bridges. They scoured these areas with a tenacity born of desperation, but as the first light of dawn broke, they were forced to return home, their search fruitless and hearts heavier.

Meanwhile, a network of friends, volunteers, and concerned citizens came together to organize a grid search that spanned a hundred-mile radius. They armed themselves with pictures of Richard's truck and its license plate, YFH-2319, covering every inch of ground they could. John even went to the extent of spending $1,200 to hire a Camden police officer and commandeer a helicopter, hoping that a bird's-eye view might reveal what was hidden on the ground. Yet, despite these Herculean efforts, the search yielded nothing but silence and unanswered questions.

A chilling interaction with a police deputy left John with a haunting statement: "No one is ever going to find anything." When John pressed for an explanation, the deputy replied, "It's too clean," hinting at the perplexing nature of the case. The absence of any leads, any traces of Danielle and Richard, or Richard's truck, was baffling. The couple seemed to have vanished without a trace.

Investigators delved into every aspect of their lives, examining bank accounts, credit card activities, and cell phone records, but all these avenues led to dead ends. No suspicious transactions or communications were uncovered. Surveillance footage from toll bridges and other potential routes provided no clues either. The couple, along with Richard's vehicle, had seemingly disappeared into thin air after leaving Abilene's bar.

One prevailing theory speculated that the couple might have accidentally driven into the nearby Delaware River. However, those acquainted with the Philadelphia area quickly pointed out flaws in this hypothesis. The geographic layout and urban planning of the area made it highly unlikely for a vehicle to inadvertently end up in the river, as there was no straightforward or direct access from the street to the water. This geographical fact significantly diminished the likelihood of the Delaware River being the scene of their disappearance.

Another theory that gained traction was the possibility of a carjacking that turned fatal, with the stolen vehicle then dismantled and sold off in a chop shop. This scenario seemed plausible, especially given the statistics: over 13,000 vehicles were reported stolen in the Philadelphia area in 2004. This alarming number indicated a not-insignificant probability of car theft, which could potentially include violent outcomes. The FBI and the Philadelphia stolen car squad collaborated to probe this angle extensively. Despite their joint efforts and expertise, this lead ultimately reached a dead end. There was no concrete evidence to support the notion of a carjacking, leaving investigators and the families without closure.

The involvement of the FBI in a missing persons case is relatively unusual, indicating the complexity and severity of this particular case. In 2014, a decade after the disappearance, FBI Special Agent Vito Roselli, leading the investigation, issued a press release that shed light on the nature of their inquiry. Agent Roselli highlighted the sheer implausibility of two people and a truck vanishing so completely and cleanly, without any witnesses or evidence, over such an extended period. He suggested that this level of precision and success in evading detection hinted at methodical planning rather than mere luck. The disturbing implication of his statement was clear: the disappearance of Danielle and Richard was likely orchestrated, a chilling and calculated act.

The FBI's assessment pointed towards a sinister possibility: a "murder-for-hire" plot. The meticulous manner in which they disappeared, leaving behind no evidence or leads, suggested a level of planning and execution that was professional and deliberate. This theory raised deeply troubling questions: Who would have the motive to orchestrate such a heinous act? What could have possibly driven someone to target Danielle and Richard in such a cold and calculated manner?

The authorities, in their quest for answers, embarked on a thorough investigation, scrutinizing every possible lead and individual connected to the couple.

Initially, the focus fell on Richard's friends, Anthony and Michelle, who were among the last to see the couple before they vanished. These individuals underwent multiple rounds of questioning, but detectives eventually concluded that neither was involved in the disappearance, closing one of the initial chapters of the investigation.

The inquiry then naturally shifted to Danielle's husband, Joe, who was scrutinized due to the strained nature of their relationship. However, Joe's alibi stood firm: he was verified to be 50 miles away at a children's birthday party, an event also attended by his stepfather, a former NYPD officer. Further complicating matters, Joe submitted to a polygraph test, but the results were inconclusive, neither implicating nor absolving him.

As the investigation deepened, unsettling revelations surfaced. It was discovered that Joe had access to Danielle's voicemail and had checked it repeatedly in the months leading up to her disappearance. Additionally, Joe was found to have made several threatening phone calls to Richard, warning him to stay away from Danielle. Despite these disturbing findings, no concrete evidence linking Joe to the couple's disappearance emerged, and he has consistently denied any involvement.

The case has seen no shortage of avenues explored and theories proposed. J.J. Klaver of the FBI encapsulated the open-ended nature of the investigation: "We're not identifying anybody as a suspect, but we're not ruling anyone out. Everybody is ruled in at this point."

One intriguing tip came from a local waitress, who reported a broken gate near the Delaware River, suggesting the possibility of a vehicle having driven through it. This led to an extensive search of the river, where several vehicles were discovered, but Richard's Dodge Dakota was not among them.

In 2021, the FBI issued a new statement, acknowledging that while the investigation had yielded some promising leads, the ultimate breakthrough, the location of Danielle and Richard or their vehicle, had eluded them.

March 2022 saw a new development as "Adventures with Purpose," a private Oregon-based search and recovery dive team, announced their involvement in the case. With an impressive track record in solving missing person cases, the team conducted multiple dives in the Delaware River, but their efforts have yet to uncover any evidence pertinent to the disappearance.

As the years pass, the families of Danielle Imbo and Richard Petrone hold onto hope, yearning for closure, for answers that would shed light on the fate of their loved ones. The mystery of their disappearance lingers, a heartbreaking reminder of the enduring quest for truth and the resilience of hope in the face of the unknown.

Suzanne Lyall

S uzanne "Suzy" Gloria Lyall, born on April 6th, 1978, in the picturesque town of Saratoga Springs, New York, emerged into a loving family headed by Doug and Mary Lyall. As the cherished youngest sibling in a family of three children, Suzy's early years were spent in the cozy community of Ballston Spa, New York, where she nurtured a deep bond with her family, especially her older brother Steven.

From a young age, Suzy was recognized as a quiet and shy individual, yet her intelligence shone brightly, particularly in her fascination with computers. Her passion for technology was not just theoretical; she possessed a remarkable ability to assemble computers from scratch, showcasing a blend of technical acumen and creativity.

Beyond her technical interests, Suzy harbored a deep love for poetry, finding solace and expression in the written word. Her father, Doug, insightfully noted, "I think it was a therapeutic way of dealing with some of the problems she was facing with her day-to-day social relationships." This artistic outlet allowed her to navigate the complexities of adolescence and personal growth.

During her high school years, Suzy's interest in technology led her to join a computer club, a decision that proved pivotal in her life. It was here that she met Richard Condon, the group's leader. The shared interests and passions soon kindled a romantic relationship between the two.

After a successful and distinguished tenure at Ballston Spa High School, where she graduated with honors in 1996, Suzy embarked on a journey of higher education. She initially attended the State University of New York (SUNY) at Oneonta to study computer science. However, seeking greater challenges and opportunities, she transferred to SUNY Albany after just one year.

To support her academic pursuits, Suzy balanced her studies with two part-time jobs. She worked at Babbage's, a software store located in the Crossgates Mall, a short distance from the university campus. Additionally, she contributed her skills to a computer company in Troy, further cementing her practical experience in the field she was so passionate about.

As a dedicated and hardworking student, Suzy Lyall maintained a rigorous routine, balancing her academic responsibilities with her job at Babbage's. Despite the challenges, she stayed in close touch with her family and Richard, her boyfriend of three years, keeping the lines of communication open through daily calls and emails. This regular contact was a testament to her strong connections and the importance she placed on her relationships.

In the early spring of 1998, Suzy faced a particularly challenging period at the university. With midterm exams on the horizon, her stress levels were understandably high. Her manager at Babbage's noticed Suzy's heightened anxiety, especially regarding one critical exam. She expressed to her manager the need to not just pass but excel in this test to uphold her impressive grade point average. This conversation highlighted Suzy's commitment to her academic pursuits and her desire to achieve excellence.

On March 1st, Suzy had a conversation with her mother, Mary, where she mentioned being low on funds and waiting for her next paycheck. Ever supportive, Mary offered to loan her some money, but Suzy, showcasing her independent spirit, declined the offer.

The day of the daunting exam, March 2nd, came, and Suzy faced it with all the preparation and determination she had. Post-exam, she felt that her performance was satisfactory, though not exceptional. Later that day, her coworker noticed that Suzy was more reserved than usual when she arrived at work, but she seemed fine otherwise. This slight change in demeanor indicated the toll that academic stress was taking on her.

Following her work shift, Suzy, as was her routine, boarded the bus to return home. The bus driver remembered picking her up that evening but could not recall the exact moment she got off. He was only certain of one thing: she was no longer on the bus when he reached the end of his route.

The last confirmed sighting of Suzy was at the Collins Circle bus stop, a brief walk from the Colonial Quad dormitory where she lived. The time was approximately 9:45 p.m. A fellow student, who knew Suzy, reported seeing her alight from the bus as they were boarding it.

After that night, the traces of Suzanne Lyall's presence vanished. She was never seen or heard from again, leaving behind a bewildered community, a distressed family, and a mystery that has persisted over time.

On the morning of March 3rd, a sense of normalcy was expected to resume in the Lyall household, but an unsettling phone call shattered that expectation. It was Richard, Suzy's boyfriend, who was on the line when Mary Lyall answered the phone. His words instantly triggered alarm: "Did you know Suzy didn't come back to campus last night?"

Richard explained, with growing concern, that Suzy hadn't replied to his calls or emails the previous night, which was completely out of character for her. Suzy was known for her consistent and timely communication, making this deviation from her usual behavior particularly alarming.

Reacting swiftly, Mary and Doug Lyall reached out to the campus security at SUNY Albany, voicing their fears and requesting an immediate check of Suzy's dorm room. The campus security initially downplayed the parents' worries, suggesting that it wasn't unusual for college students to have unexplained absences. Nevertheless, they acceded to the request and conducted an inspection of Suzy's room.

Upon examination, Suzy's room appeared normal, with no obvious signs of disturbance or foul play. However, the most glaring and distressing sign was Suzy's absence. Mary later described the scene: "When the dorm was looked at later, it looked as if she was coming back. Her hair dryer was on the bed, all her personal items were still there. She had money on top of her desk, change." This observation painted a picture of a routine day interrupted, with personal belongings left as if their owner intended to return shortly.

Further inquiries revealed that no one could recall seeing Suzy return to the campus on the evening of March 2nd. The last confirmed sighting of her was at the bus stop near the campus, leaving a trail that abruptly went cold.

The question of what happened to Suzy after she left the bus stop loomed large. Did she encounter someone before she could reach her dormitory? These questions, laden with possibilities and devoid of answers, continue to haunt those who knew her, even decades later.

Initially, campus police maintained a stance of nonchalance, convinced that Suzy would reappear of her own accord. However, as Suzy missed a crucial midterm exam and her classes in the subsequent days — behavior utterly uncharacteristic of the diligent and dependable student — the seriousness of the situation dawned on them. They commenced an investigation and sought assistance from the New York State Police.

In a collective effort to uncover the truth, the Lyalls and SUNY Albany announced a reward of $15,000 for information that could lead to Suzy's whereabouts. This move signified not just a desperate plea for leads, but also the community's profound concern for one of their own.

Further investigation into Suzy's movements revealed that her key card, essential for accessing various buildings on campus, including her dormitory, had not been used since the afternoon of March 2nd. This detail indicated that she hadn't returned to campus after her last known sighting, deepening the mystery surrounding her whereabouts.

Seeking more clues, Mary and Doug Lyall turned their attention to Suzy's banking activities. They discovered that three withdrawals had been made from her bank account between March 2nd and 3rd. The first two, occurring before her disappearance, were both for $20, a sum Suzy typically withdrew. However, Mary found it unusual that Suzy would make two withdrawals on the same day, a deviation from her usual pattern, and this anomaly remained unexplained.

The third withdrawal, made on March 3rd, the day after Suzy vanished, was from an ATM at a Stewart's Shops in Albany and was again for $20. Intriguingly, law enforcement doubted that Suzy had made this withdrawal herself.

The question then arose: who else knew her PIN? Richard, Suzy's boyfriend, claimed that only he and Suzy knew it. The reason for Richard having her PIN remains unclear.

Around the same time as this mysterious withdrawal, a man, later dubbed "Nike man" due to the hat he wore, was seen in the Stewart's Shops. He was identified and questioned by police, who were eager to determine if there was any connection to Suzy's disappearance. After thorough interrogation, law enforcement concluded that his presence was coincidental and he likely had no involvement, though they couldn't completely exclude him as a suspect.

The identity of the individual who made the third withdrawal and their motive remained shrouded in mystery.

The Lyall family, grappling with the unsettling reality, understood that Suzy was not one to act impulsively. She was a person of routine, unlikely to leave without notice, especially for an extended period. Her close relationship with her family and her habit of daily communication further emphasized that her disappearance was out of character. Suzy's consistent attendance at classes and her commitment to exams reinforced this belief.

Doug Lyall, reflecting on the situation, expressed a grave realization: "I knew something awful had happened. Suzy was not a risk taker. She didn't party or use drugs or alcohol." Her cautious nature, coupled with the fact that she did not drive and relied solely on public transportation, painted a picture of a young woman unlikely to suddenly vanish without a trace.

Two months after her disappearance, a disconcerting clue emerged: Suzy's Babbage's name tag was found in the parking lot, about 90 feet from the bus stop. Intriguingly, it was located on the opposite side of the lot, leading away from her dormitory. Adding to the enigma, it was an older name tag, not the one she had been using at the time she went missing.

In the aftermath, a massive effort was undertaken to find Suzy. Investigators pursued an impressive 270 leads and meticulously combed through approximately 300 acres of surrounding land, including dense wooded areas and the expansive waters of nearby Rensselaer Lake. These extensive searches, conducted in the weeks following her disappearance, were a testament to the seriousness with which her case was treated.

Despite these efforts, the investigation soon ground to a halt, hampered by a lack of conclusive evidence. The trail seemed to grow cold, leaving authorities and Suzy's loved ones in a state of frustrating uncertainty.

A potentially significant development emerged when one of Suzy's coworkers at Babbage's reported that she had mentioned being stalked by an unknown individual prior to her disappearance. Intriguingly, Suzy did not seem to express fear of this individual. The identity of this alleged stalker has never been uncovered, adding another unanswered question to the growing list.

The case also cast a spotlight on Richard, Suzy's boyfriend, who became a person of interest for several reasons. Mary Lyall, Suzy's mother, viewed Richard with suspicion. He was not only one of the few people who knew Suzy's PIN number but also reportedly had a tumultuous relationship with her.

Richard was described as controlling and manipulative by some accounts. Mary revealed that Suzy was unhappy with the relationship and had attempted to end it multiple times, each time penning a letter to Richard. These breakup attempts would invariably result in Richard becoming emotional and persuading Suzy to remain in the relationship.

Adding to the suspicion, Richard, who lived a mere 10 minutes from Suzy's campus, did not check on her in her dorm room or contact the police when he failed to hear from her. Additionally, he had remote access to her computer, though the purpose of this access remains unclear.

A poignant detail shared by Mary involved a visit to Suzy's grandmother in February. During the trip, Suzy wanted to stop by Richard's place to give him a Valentine's Day card. Mary speculated that this card might have been another attempt by Suzy to end the relationship, but the true contents of the card remain known only to Richard. There was also speculation about whether Suzy might have been seeing someone else, though no evidence has emerged to support this theory.

Richard, on his part, maintained that their relationship was strong, even claiming they were engaged, a detail that came as a surprise to Suzy's friends and family, as she had never mentioned any engagement.

Initially cooperative with the investigation, Richard informed law enforcement that he had been home playing an online game with a friend on the night Suzy disappeared, an alibi corroborated by the friend. However, he later retained a lawyer, refused a polygraph test, and ceased further cooperation with investigators.

While police found his alibi relatively satisfactory, they have never been able to definitively exclude Richard as a suspect. Nonetheless, it's important to note that no evidence has been found linking him to Suzy's disappearance.

The investigation took a new turn in 2005. Investigators began to focus their attention on John Regan, a man who had emerged as a person of interest. Regan's arrest in 2005 for the attempted abduction of a female student at Saratoga Springs High School, not far from Suzy's hometown of Ballston Spa, raised suspicions. His criminal record was further tainted by charges related to a 1993 kidnapping case in Connecticut, adding to the concerns about his potential involvement in Suzy's case.

Despite the growing interest in his possible connection to Suzy's disappearance, Regan remained silent, refusing to discuss the case with the police. The link, if any, between Regan and Suzy's case remained elusive, as investigators found no concrete evidence to implicate him.

In the ensuing years, a new theory emerged, involving one of America's most notorious serial killers, Israel Keyes. Keyes, who resided in Constable, New York, in 1998, lived approximately 3.5 hours from Suzy's college in Albany. Notably, Keyes would later enlist in the army in Albany the same year, a detail that drew the attention of those scrutinizing Suzy's case.

Keyes' known modus operandi in other crimes bore some similarities to aspects of Suzy's disappearance. He was known to have demanded a victim's PIN number and used her debit card for withdrawals, a detail that echoed the mysterious ATM withdrawal in Suzy's case. Additionally, his habit of scouting potential victims in parking lots paralleled the location where Suzy's name tag was found.

This led to speculation: could Keyes have been the unknown individual allegedly stalking Suzy? The possibility was chilling but remained speculative.

Keyes' arrest in 2012, followed by his suicide in prison in December of the same year, left many questions unanswered. Although he was confirmed to have killed three people, his suicide note and other indications suggested he could have been responsible for up to 11 murders. However, the lack of specifics regarding the identities of these victims meant that any connection to Suzy's case would remain in the realm of speculation.

Keyes' internet search history, which included a list dubbed "NAMUS-45" featuring missing persons including Suzy, added an intriguing angle to the theory. While the list's significance as evidence was limited, as some names could be definitively or reasonably excluded as his victims, it did add a layer of intrigue when combined with the circumstantial details of Suzy's disappearance.

The enduring pain and uncertainty following Suzy Lyall's disappearance galvanized her parents, Doug and Mary Lyall, into action. Their tireless efforts culminated in a significant legislative achievement known as "Suzanne's Law." Signed by President George W. Bush in 2003, this law marked a crucial step in improving the response to missing persons cases. It mandates that police immediately report to the National Crime Information Center (NCIC) when anyone aged 18 to 21 is reported missing, a protocol that was not followed in Suzy's case.

Beyond their legislative triumph, Doug and Mary Lyall also established The Center For Hope. This organization emerged as a beacon of support, offering assistance and solidarity to families grappling with the anguish of having a missing loved one. Their unwavering dedication to this cause underscored their commitment to transforming personal tragedy into a source of hope for others.

Despite the passage of time, the Lyall family's resolve to find Suzy and provide her with a dignified resting place remained unshaken. They clung to the hope that one day they would uncover the truth about what happened to their beloved daughter and sister.

Tragically, Doug Lyall passed away in 2015 without the closure and answers he had long sought. His departure was not just a personal loss to the family but also a poignant reminder of the unresolved nature of Suzy's case.

Mary Lyall, however, continues to champion the cause, driven by a mix of maternal love and the unyielding desire for truth. Her words poignantly capture the depth of her grief: "You can never get over it. There's always that hole in your heart. It'll never heal. It's the worst thing that could ever happen to a parent."

Richard, Suzy's former boyfriend, has remained silent about her disappearance. According to his family, he has moved on, now married and leading a different life.

Reflecting on the state of the investigation in 2018, former lead investigator John Camp shared his perspective, "We believe it's a homicide. Is there a chance she moved away? It's a possibility, but the reality is she's probably been a victim of a homicide."

Despite the passing years, there have been no recent breakthroughs in the investigation, which continues actively. The mystery of what transpired on that chilly March evening in 1998, leading to the disappearance of 19-year-old Suzanne Lyall, remains unsolved, a haunting and unresolved chapter in the annals of criminal history.

Tiffany Daniels

Tiffany Daniels, a Dallas native, made a lasting impression during her high school years with her vibrant interest in the arts and her effervescent personality. Known for being exceptionally free-spirited, her family often reminisced about her unique ability to uplift those around her with her mere presence. Tiffany's passion for painting led her to a fulfilling job at Pensacola State College theater in Pensacola, Florida, where she skillfully painted sets, blending her work with her artistic inclinations.

Outside her professional life, Daniels fully immersed herself in the rich cultural and natural offerings of Pensacola. In the heart of the city's downtown, just a stone's throw away from her workplace, she was a familiar face at blues and swing dance parties, often taking the lead in organizing these vibrant events. Her residence, conveniently located near the Bob Sikes Bridge leading to the picturesque Santa Rosa Island in the Gulf of Mexico, served as a gateway to her outdoor adventures. Tiffany frequently explored the scenic dunes through hiking and biking. Embracing a pescetarian lifestyle, she expressed her love for nature through a series of tattoos on her feet, artistically depicting the stages of a plant's growth and bloom.

However, beneath the surface of her seemingly content life, Tiffany grappled with financial challenges. According to her parents, they began to notice in the summer of 2013 a troubling pattern: Tiffany often ended up covering rent for a succession of housemates who were either unwilling or unable to contribute their share. This recurring issue came to a head in July that year when, following the departure of another roommate, she turned to Craigslist to find a new housemate.

Gary Nichols, a 54-year-old man undergoing a separation from his wife and seeking to live closer to his workplace, responded to Tiffany's ad. As the father of one of her friends, Nichols shared several common interests with Daniels, including a penchant for bicycling and a similar dietary preference. Despite the considerable age difference, which initially caused some concern for Tiffany's parents, Gary proved to be a responsible roommate, consistently meeting his share of the living expenses.

On the memorable morning of August 11, Tiffany Daniels commenced her day with a bittersweet note, hosting a farewell breakfast for her boyfriend. This was a significant day for him, as he had recently been accepted into the prestigious graduate robotics program at the University of Texas in Austin. He had proposed that Tiffany join him in Austin, a suggestion that she contemplated with mixed feelings. Tiffany's friends shared that while her love for him remained strong, and she even eagerly made plans to visit him later in Austin, she wasn't ready to leave her life in Pensacola behind. The breakfast was a blend of farewells and future promises, and after the meal, her boyfriend departed, leaving Tiffany in a state of reflective melancholy.

The rest of Tiffany's day was shadowed by a hint of sadness from the morning's goodbye, yet it was also laced with an undercurrent of excitement about her upcoming visit to Austin. Austin was a city her friends believed she would find appealing and easy to adapt to, given its vibrant culture and artistic pulse. Tiffany and the theater department at her job were gearing up for a new project: preparing sets for a production of "Spamalot" that fall. This new endeavor offered her a creative outlet and a distraction from her personal life.

To draw inspiration for the project and to find some relaxation, that night Tiffany and her roommate, Gary Nichols, decided to watch "Monty Python and the Holy Grail." This classic film was the basis for the musical "Spamalot," and watching it served a dual purpose - a source of creative ideas and a means to unwind. Following the movie, both retreated to their respective bedrooms, mindful of their early work commitments the next morning.

In the quiet of the early hours, around 5 a.m., Nichols recalled a peculiar occurrence. He heard the door of the house open and close several times. Curious and slightly concerned, he peered outside from his room, half-expecting to see Tiffany, but she was nowhere in sight.

Later, as Nichols left for work around 7 a.m., he noticed Tiffany's car, a gray Toyota 4Runner, was not in its usual spot. He naturally assumed Tiffany had left for work early, an unusual occurrence for her. Tiffany's parents later commented that it was out of character for her to wake up early; she typically timed her mornings so she would leave just in time to reach her destination.

Tiffany Daniels began her workday as usual, punctually arriving to paint sets, a task she approached with her characteristic creativity and dedication. However, on this particular day, there was a noticeable deviation in her routine. She approached her supervisor with a request to leave a bit earlier than usual. Additionally, she mentioned her plan to take some time off, possibly for the entire week. Her reasons were vague, framed simply as "things she had to take care of." Her supervisor, understanding the occasional need for personal time, agreed to her request. Thus, at 4:43 p.m., Tiffany clocked out and left the theater. Little did anyone know, this would be the last confirmed sighting of her.

As the evening progressed, Gary Nichols, her roommate, started to feel a growing sense of unease. By 10 p.m., Tiffany had not returned home, an unusual occurrence given her typical routine. Her continued absence, coupled with her unresponsiveness to his calls, deepened Nichols' concern. He reached out to his daughter Noel for advice. Noel, trying to assuage her father's worries, suggested that Tiffany, as an independent adult, might simply be spending time with friends closer to her age group. Nichols, though not fully convinced, decided to follow his daughter's reasoning and retired to bed.

The next morning brought no relief to Nichols' concerns. Tiffany's continued absence and the lack of response to his calls compounded the worry. The situation took a more serious turn that evening when Nichols returned home to discover that the electricity to the house had been shut off. Jumping to the conclusion that Tiffany might have neglected to pay her share of the bills, he once again contacted his daughter to inform her of the situation and Tiffany's ongoing absence. This time, his tone was more urgent. He suggested that Noel should reach out to Tiffany's parents, a step that marked the escalation of their concerns. Noel heeded her father's advice and sent a private Facebook message to Tiffany's mother, Cindy.

Cindy, along with Noel, began an exhaustive search through Tiffany's network of friends, hoping to uncover some clue to her whereabouts. However, their inquiries led nowhere; none of Tiffany's friends had seen her that week. They shared a common assumption that she might be visiting other acquaintances, but this possibility was quickly dismissed as Cindy and Noel had already contacted them. As the week drew to a close without any sign of Tiffany, the gravity of the situation became undeniable. It was time to involve the authorities. Cindy and Noel made the difficult decision to report Tiffany Daniels as missing, initiating an official search that would soon capture the attention and concern of the wider community.

Cindy Daniels, deeply concerned about her daughter Tiffany's sudden and unexplained disappearance, took her first step by visiting the Escambia County sheriff's office. However, her initial interaction there left her feeling disheartened. She sensed a certain dismissiveness from the officials; they recorded the details she provided but seemed to harbor the belief that Tiffany had simply gone out partying and would soon return on her own. Their casual approach to what Cindy felt was a serious matter added to her distress. However, a jurisdictional technicality shifted the case's focus: since Tiffany lived and was last seen in the city of Pensacola, the responsibility for investigating her disappearance fell to the Pensacola police department. Cindy noted a marked difference in their approach; they exhibited a greater sense of urgency and concern about the case.

Detective Daniel Harnett, assigned to Tiffany's case, met with Cindy at her daughter's house to conduct a thorough search. The investigation inside the house revealed no immediate signs of struggle or foul play. A significant observation was that Tiffany's tent, an item she would likely take if planning a camping trip, remained untouched in her room. This detail led Harnett to deduce that if Tiffany had decided to leave town, it wasn't for a camping adventure.

The detective's investigation took a new direction when he learned about Tiffany's boyfriend leaving Pensacola for Austin the day before her disappearance. This detail piqued Harnett's interest, and he delved into exploring this lead. The boyfriend, upon being contacted, was cooperative. He had called Tiffany upon his arrival in Austin on the 11th but had no contact with her on the 12th. His willingness to provide fingerprints and DNA samples, along with cell phone records confirming his presence in Austin throughout the weekend, effectively ruled him out as having clandestinely returned to Pensacola.

Another angle Harnett considered was the emotional impact of the boyfriend's departure on Tiffany. Her sister, in an interview with the show "Disappeared," mentioned that Tiffany had seemed slightly less spirited earlier in 2013. However, Tiffany had been making future plans — not only the trip to Austin but also organizing a dance event in two weeks. This suggested that she wasn't in a state of mind to either harm herself or start anew elsewhere.

During the investigation, it was discovered that after leaving work early, Tiffany had briefly returned to her house. Nichols, her roommate, was at home during that time, engaged in a phone conversation with his out-of-state girlfriend. However, he did not recall noticing Tiffany's presence. Cindy expressed skepticism about Nichols' lack of awareness, particularly because of the open space between the top of Tiffany's closet wall and his statement about hearing the front door open and close in the morning. Despite these doubts, the police believed Nichols' account and did not consider him a suspect, noting his role in initially raising concerns about Tiffany's whereabouts.

As the first weekend after her disappearance unfolded, the media caught wind of the story, broadcasting it across various news channels. Simultaneously, Tiffany's friends and family mobilized in a remarkable display of community effort. They blanketed the streets with fliers and posted them everywhere possible, their determination fueled by the hope of finding any clue that could lead to Tiffany.

This extensive publicity effort soon yielded a significant breakthrough. On August 20, a mere eight days after Tiffany was last seen, a jogger, who happened to be acquainted with Tiffany's family, made a crucial discovery. In the parking lot at Park West, near Fort Pickens at the western end of Santa Rosa Island, Tiffany's 4Runner was spotted. The location was familiar; Tiffany often ventured to the nearby dunes of Gulf Islands National Seashore for hiking, despite her mother Cindy's warnings about the risks of visiting the beach alone. The discovery of the car in such a location sent a chill down Cindy's spine, as it seemed to confirm her worst fears about her daughter's fate.

When the police arrived and towed the 4Runner to their garage for a detailed examination, they uncovered several intriguing items inside: Tiffany's bicycle, cell phone, purse with her wallet, some clothes, her paintings, a jug of water, and a jar of peanut butter. However, the investigation took a perplexing turn when two fingerprints were found – one on the door handle and the other on the steering wheel – neither of which matched Tiffany or any of the investigators who had handled the car.

Adding to the mystery, a resident from a nearby condominium asserted that the car had not been in the lot until two days prior to its discovery. This statement was further complicated by the accounts of two other residents who claimed to have seen a man exiting the car earlier that day.

Detective Harnett, in an attempt to piece together the timeline of events, turned to security camera footage from the toll booths at the Bob Sikes Bridge, the only road connection between Pensacola and the island. The footage revealed a critical piece of the puzzle: Tiffany's 4Runner had crossed the toll at 7:51 p.m. on the day she vanished. However, the footage was inconclusive regarding who was driving the car at that time.

As the case stands, Tiffany's 4Runner remains in the police impound lot, with its contents undisturbed. The authorities have preserved it as a vital piece of evidence, holding onto the hope that new information may surface.

Given the location's proximity to two large residential complexes frequented by the island's summer vacationers, it was plausible that a resident or visitor might have noticed something pertinent. Driven by a mix of hope and urgency, Tiffany's friends and family reinvigorated their efforts. They distributed flyers extensively in the area and went door-to-door, engaging with residents in a thorough canvassing operation. Despite their exhaustive efforts, this line of inquiry yielded no tangible leads.

Meanwhile, at the police garage, a curious detail emerged. Investigators found sand on the bicycle tires inside Tiffany's 4Runner, but notably, there was no sand on the car's floorboards. This discovery led Detective Harnett to consider a new possibility: if Tiffany had indeed gone for a bike ride on the beach that fateful evening, she might have subsequently decided to take a swim. This theory was bolstered by a friend's reminder that the Perseid meteor shower was occurring around that time, an astronomical event Tiffany might have been drawn to watch from the beach. If she had ventured into the water, it raised the grim possibility of drowning. However, the absence of any bodies washing up on the shore, a common occurrence after a drowning, made this scenario less likely.

Another unsettling possibility was that Tiffany might have encountered an accident or foul play on land. The vastness of Santa Rosa Island, stretching over 50 miles, posed a significant challenge. The island's varied terrain, with its expansive beaches and areas of dense vegetation, required extensive manpower to search - resources the police simply did not have.

In a concerted effort the weekend following the car's discovery, KlaasKids, a volunteer search organization established in the wake of the Polly Klaas case, collaborated with local police and the U.S. National Park Service, which oversees the National Seashore. This large-scale search involved both human searchers and dogs, meticulously combing much of the island. While they did uncover some fragments of clothing and pieces of jewelry, none of these items were linked to Tiffany Daniels.

In an effort to expand the reach of their search, they established a Facebook page dedicated to finding Tiffany. This page quickly became a hub for tips and leads, with many individuals coming forward with potential sightings and information. Among these, a tip from a convenience store clerk initially seemed promising. The clerk claimed to have seen Tiffany several days after her last known appearance, even noting her distinctive foot tattoos. However, this lead hit a dead end when the store's security footage from that day failed to confirm the clerk's account.

Months later, in January 2014, the Facebook page produced what Tiffany's parents considered a more credible lead. A waitress at a restaurant in Metairie, Louisiana, near New Orleans, reported an intriguing sighting. She recalled serving a woman who bore a striking resemblance to Tiffany, accompanied by two other women — one about the same age and the other older, possibly Latina, and more elegantly dressed. The waitress noted peculiar behavior from the younger women; they wore long-sleeved shirts despite the heat, with the cuffs pulled down over their hands, and avoided eye contact. The group largely communicated through the older woman. When the waitress mentioned the resemblance to the missing woman from Florida, the trio abruptly left the restaurant. Unfortunately, any chance of verifying this encounter was lost as the restaurant's security footage had since been overwritten.

Tiffany's parents found this account particularly compelling for two reasons. Firstly, Tiffany had a habit of pulling her sleeves over her hands when she felt cold, a distinctive mannerism noted by the waitress. Secondly, the waitress mentioned that the woman resembling Tiffany inquired about whether a soup used fish or chicken broth. This detail resonated with Cindy, Tiffany's mother, who remembered a similar incident where Tiffany, a pescetarian, could discern the substitution of chicken broth in her soup.

This sighting, combined with the lack of progress in the search, led the Daniels family to a harrowing consideration. They began to fear that Tiffany might have been taken out of Pensacola against her will during the week between her last confirmed sighting and the commencement of the search. The family delved into the grim world of human trafficking as a potential explanation. They drew parallels between Tiffany's case and that of another woman from nearby Panama City, who had been drugged, abducted, and taken to New Orleans to work as a prostitute.

While human traffickers typically target younger women, Tiffany's parents believed that she could have been an exception due to her trusting nature. They noted that Interstate 10, connecting Pensacola and New Orleans, is often cited as a major trafficking route in the U.S. Detective Harnett, however, maintained that while the police had found no concrete evidence to support the trafficking theory, they had not ruled out any possibilities in this complex and ongoing case.

As the two-year mark of Tiffany Daniels' mysterious disappearance approached in 2015, the case witnessed two significant developments, rekindling public interest and hope for new leads. The Investigation Discovery (ID) cable network, recognizing the compelling nature of Tiffany's story, chose to feature her case in the revival of its series "Disappeared." This show, known for its in-depth exploration of missing-persons cases, offered a new platform to bring national attention to Tiffany's disappearance. The ID crew traveled to Pensacola, capturing the essence of the case through filming at key locations associated with Tiffany's life and disappearance. They recreated certain scenes to offer viewers a closer look into the events leading up to her vanishing. In their pursuit of a comprehensive narrative, the crew conducted interviews with Detective Harnett, Tiffany's parents, her sister, and friends who had been deeply involved in the investigation. The episode, which aired in April 2016, brought renewed focus to the case, reaching a wide audience and inviting fresh perspectives.

Before this episode was broadcasted, a new piece of evidence emerged, reinvigorating the investigation. In December 2015, following increased media coverage around the second anniversary of Tiffany's disappearance, a significant lead was brought to the attention of the Daniels family and the police. A citizen stepped forward with a crucial observation from the day Tiffany's car was found. They reported seeing a man in his thirties, clad in red shorts and shirtless, opening the car's tailgate. This description aligned with the statements of two other witnesses who had previously mentioned seeing a man leaving Tiffany's car after it was parked. The witness's account was particularly noteworthy because they remembered the incident clearly due to the car being parked unusually, facing against the traffic flow, in an area typically reserved for wildlife. This new information added a mysterious dimension to the case, suggesting the involvement of an unidentified individual on the day Tiffany's car was discovered.

In a poignant tribute to Tiffany and to keep her memory alive in the public consciousness, a mural was created around the 10th anniversary of her disappearance. This mural, painted on Pensacola's famous Graffiti Bridge, depicted Tiffany's image and served as a vivid reminder of her case. It stood as a symbol of the community's continued hope and commitment to finding answers about Tiffany Daniels' fate, a testament to the enduring impact of her disappearance on the Pensacola community and beyond.

Bryce Laspisa

Bryce David Laspisa's life story unfolds in the quiet, family-oriented suburb of Naperville, Illinois, just outside the bustling city of Chicago. Raised as the cherished only child in a small, nurturing family, Bryce's early years were marked by a warm and supportive environment.

From a young age, Bryce's creative talents were evident. He had a natural flair for art, often seen with a pencil or brush in hand, creating vivid drawings that showcased his budding artistic skills. Alongside his love for art, Bryce was a passionate gamer, spending hours mastering various games on his Xbox, a hobby that brought him immense joy and relaxation.

In school, Bryce's intelligence and charisma shone brightly. He was not only academically gifted, excelling in his studies, but also possessed a magnetic personality that made him popular among his peers. His father, Michael, fondly remembers Bryce as a social butterfly, always surrounded by friends and actively involved in various activities.

His mother, Karen, echoes this sentiment, adding that Bryce was exceptionally communicative and open-hearted, traits he seemingly inherited from her. "He would talk to [us] about any subject," she reminisced, emphasizing how Bryce was an 'open book,' comfortable in sharing his thoughts and feelings with his parents.

The Laspisa family, close-knit and loving, shared a bond that was the envy of many. Bryce, in particular, felt deeply connected to his parents, often sharing his life's minutiae with them. Or at least, that's what his parents believed.

Upon his parents' retirement, the Laspisa family embarked on a new chapter, moving from the familiar surroundings of Naperville to the sun-soaked shores of California. They settled in Laguna Niguel, an upscale beach community in Orange County, seeking a peaceful life under the Californian sun. This move coincided with a significant milestone in Bryce's life - his high school graduation in 2012.

As Bryce stepped into adulthood, he pursued his academic and creative passions by enrolling in Sierra College in Rocklin. This college, located about seven hours north of his new home in Laguna Niguel, offered him an opportunity to delve deeper into graphic and industrial design, fields that resonated with his artistic inclinations.

During his first term at college, Bryce's life took a romantic turn when he met Kim Sly, a fellow student. This new relationship marked the beginning of a significant phase in his life, as Bryce navigated the challenges and joys of young adulthood, college life, and a budding romance.

During the warm months of 2013, an unsettling shift began to occur in Bryce Laspisa's life, one that raised concerns among those closest to him. His girl-friend Kim and his roommate Sean, who had become a close confidant, started to notice changes in his behavior, particularly his increasing indulgence in alcohol.

Bryce, at 19, had also started using Vyvanse, an amphetamine typically prescribed for ADHD and binge-eating disorder. It was unclear how Bryce, who didn't have a prescription, got hold of this medication. According to some reports, he began using Vyvanse to extend his gaming sessions late into the night, a decision that would have significant repercussions.

The side effects of Vyvanse, especially when combined with alcohol, can be severe. They include symptoms like headaches, dizziness, racing heartbeats, hallucinations, nausea, sleep disturbances, and irritability. Bryce's decision to mix alcohol with Vyvanse set off alarm bells among his friends, who saw this as a dangerous path.

As the summer of 2013 waned, Bryce's behavior grew increasingly erratic and worrisome. In a series of actions that seemed out of character, Bryce began giving away his possessions, including his beloved Xbox and a cherished pair of diamond earrings, a heartfelt gift from his mother. These giveaways were accompanied by a cryptic and emotional text to Sean, expressing deep affection and gratitude, hinting at an internal turmoil: "I love you, bro, seriously. You're the best person I've ever met. You saved my soul."

His relationships also began to fracture. Bryce unexpectedly ended his relationship with Kim, suggesting that she would be better off without him. This breakup, abrupt and unexplained, only added to the growing concerns about his state of mind.

In the midst of this turmoil, Bryce expressed a desire to return home and speak with his parents, hinting at something significant he needed to discuss. Kim, deeply worried by his condition and recent actions, took his car keys in an attempt to prevent him from driving. When she contacted Bryce's parents, explaining her concerns and hesitance to let him drive, Bryce downplayed the situation, implying that Kim was simply upset about their breakup.

During a phone conversation with his mother, Karen, Bryce's words were tinged with ambiguity and urgency. Karen later recalled, "I said 'Bryce, I'm worried. Let me come up there tomorrow. Let me fly up there tomorrow,' and he says 'Mom, no. Don't make any airline reservations until I talk to you because I have a lot to talk to you about.'"

This conversation, filled with unspoken words and concerns, would be the last time Karen and Michael Laspisa heard their son express a desire to share something significant with them. Despite his assurances that he was fine, the unease hung heavily in the air. Eventually, Karen, hoping to trust her son's judgment, persuaded Kim to return his keys. Bryce left Kim's place around 11:30 p.m., claiming he was heading back to his apartment.

On that fateful evening, Christian realized he had missed a call from Karen. Concerned, he promptly returned the call, only to discover that her son Bryce was still not home. Eager to help, Christian offered to search for Bryce and keep Karen updated on his whereabouts.

Christian's search efforts paid off when he found Bryce at the very location where the police had previously encountered him. He advised Bryce to start his journey home, offering to follow him in his vehicle for safety. Bryce agreed, and Christian trailed behind him for 10 miles, ensuring he was safely on Interstate 5, before stopping to inform Karen of her son's progress.

As the night deepened, Bryce paused his journey at 12:30 a.m. for a brief stop to refuel his car and grab a soda. However, when Karen attempted to reach him twenty minutes later, her calls went unanswered.

Finally, at 1:50 a.m., Bryce responded to his parents' call. His replies were elusive and vague, frustrating their efforts to pinpoint his exact location. He cited the absence of signs and the enveloping darkness as reasons for his inability to provide clear details.

Attempting to alleviate their concerns, Bryce shared that his GPS estimated his arrival home at 3:25 a.m. He last spoke with his parents at 2:09 a.m., informing them of his plan to pull over for a nap, a decision they supported given his apparent exhaustion.

The next morning brought a chilling twist to the story. The Laspisas were startled awake by their doorbell, expecting to see Bryce. Instead, they were greeted by a California Highway Patrol officer, who inquired about a 2003 beige Toyota Highlander. This vehicle, belonging to Bryce, was found at the bottom of a 25-foot embankment near Castaic Lake at 5:30 a.m., lying on its side with a shattered rear windshield. The officer theorized that Bryce had escaped through the broken window after the crash.

Inside the abandoned SUV were Bryce's wallet, cell phone, and laptop. A small amount of Bryce's blood was discovered on the headrest and backseat, suggesting minor injuries, though the possibility of more serious internal damage could not be ruled out.

Strangely, Bryce was nowhere to be found. Nearby, an unzipped duffel bag hinted at his hasty departure, leaving behind his valuables in a shroud of mystery.

An examination of the tire tracks revealed a disturbing detail: Bryce had accelerated down the hill, igniting speculation about his intentions in causing the crash.

The search for Bryce Laspisa unfolded like a meticulously orchestrated operation, encompassing a wide array of resources and techniques. The search teams, a blend of determination and expertise, included officers navigating the rugged terrain on foot, horseback, and all-terrain four-wheelers. The operation was further bolstered by the inclusion of specialized teams – divers plunged into the depths of Castaic Lake, bloodhounds followed the faintest of scents, and cadaver dogs, trained to uncover the most concealed clues, were all part of this extensive search.

In a significant development, K9 units successfully tracked Bryce's scent along Lake Hughes Road, leading them to a gas station and truck stop. Intriguingly, this is where the trail went cold, raising perplexing questions. Had Bryce been picked up by someone at this location? The mystery deepened, leaving the search teams and Bryce's family grappling with numerous possibilities.

Despite the relentless efforts that spanned several days, the search in and around Castaic Lake, known for its daunting depth of 300 feet, yielded no tangible results. Bryce remained elusive, his whereabouts a mystery that the lake's depths refused to reveal.

In a twist that added to the complex puzzle, security camera footage provided a narrow window into Bryce's movements. The footage captured him driving down Lake Hughes Road at 2:15 a.m., shortly after he had informed his mother of his intention to take a nap. In a curious recurrence, he was seen once again at 4:29 a.m., traversing the same road. Beyond these fleeting appearances, Bryce's vehicle vanished from the camera's eye, deepening the enigma of his disappearance.

The search took a grim turn on September 4th, 2013. Responding to reports of a fire near Castaic Lake, in the vicinity of Bryce's last known whereabouts, police made a harrowing discovery – charred human remains. This development sent ripples of expectation and dread; many braced for the possibility that these remains might be Bryce's. However, in a twist that only compounded the mystery, it was determined that the remains were not his.

This revelation, while offering a momentary glimmer of hope, also plunged the search into deeper uncertainty. The quest to unravel the fate of Bryce Laspisa continued, each passing day adding layers to a mystery that seemed to grow more profound and perplexing.

The mysterious case of Bryce Laspisa took a new turn when his parents, Karen and Michael, unsatisfied with the official response to their son's disappearance, hired a private investigator. Despite her thorough efforts, she was unable to uncover any new leads. Her hypothesis suggested that Bryce might have suffered a head injury during the accident, potentially resulting in amnesia or a fugue state, which could explain why he vanished so suddenly.

In their relentless search for answers, Bryce's parents took another significant step in 2015. They engaged a sonar specialist to conduct a detailed search of Castaic Lake. However, this advanced effort yielded no new information regarding Bryce's whereabouts.

Throughout the years following Bryce's disappearance, various unconfirmed sightings have been reported from states like Oregon, California, and Texas. Yet, there has been no activity on Bryce's bank account, credit cards, Social Security number, or passport since he went missing.

Initially, police considered the possibility that Bryce might have committed suicide, given his behavior prior to his disappearance. They also speculated that he might have chosen to start a new life elsewhere. However, his parents have always dismissed the idea that Bryce would intentionally leave his life and family. Karen emphasized, "He never ran away from home... He loved us too much and we love him too."

In 2022, a significant development occurred. The "Find Bryce Laspisa" Facebook page reported what seemed to be a credible sighting of Bryce in Missoula, Montana. A photo showing a man remarkably similar to an older, disheveled Bryce captured the public's attention. Detective Ethan Smith followed this lead, but after investigating, he confirmed that the man was not Bryce. The resemblance was striking, but it was a false alarm.

The circumstances of what happened to Bryce after his accident and the issues he faced in the days before he went missing continue to be a mystery. Police now believe that Bryce did not die from his injuries in the accident. Considering his past substance abuse and erratic behavior, it's speculated that he might have experienced a psychotic break and could be living off-grid in a distressed mental state. This theory leaves his family and supporters in a state of unresolved hope, as the quest for the truth about Bryce's fate continues.

Bibliography

Blietz, Lena. "In 1974, Three Fort Worth Girls Vanished. Forty Years Later, This Is All We Know." Fort Worth Star-Telegram, 20 Dec. 2017.

Burbeck, Tony. "After 15 years, family keeps searching for Asha Degree." WCNC, 12 Feb. 2015.

Clarridge, Christine. "Sky Metalwala's disappearance still an active investigation after 3 years." Seattle Times, 7 Nov. 2014.

Corbin, Cristina. "Two years later, mystery surrounds disappearance of Indiana University student Lauren Spierer." Fox News, 1 June 2013.

Dunn, Morgan. "The Story Of Bryce Laspisa And His Chilling Disappearance In California." All That Is Interesting, 23 Jan. 2023.

Fiorello, Victor. "It's Been 11 Years Since Danielle Imbo and Richard Petrone Vanished." Philadelphia Magazine, 10 Feb. 2016.

Gore, Donna. "The Legacy of Leah Toby Roberts and the 'On the Road to Remember Tour' with the CUE Center for Missing Persons 2014." 17 Aug. 2014.

Harlow, Jadyn. "The Disappearance of Asha Degree: A Two Decades Long Valentines Day Mystery." Medium, 5 Feb. 2023.

Haynes, Mark. "Missing man mystery: 'None of it makes sense,' Steven Koecher's mother laments." Salt Lake Tribune, 8 Jan. 2010.

Haynes, Mark. "Utahn Steven Koecher's disappearance remains a mystery." Salt Lake Tribune, 12 Dec. 2011.

Hedda, Benjamin. "Missing: All Theories On How Sneha Philip Vanished." Screen Rant, 18 Dec. 2022.

Johnson, Krista. "The mystery around the disappearance of Brandon Lawson." San Angelo Standard-Times, 12 July 2018.

Lang, Alex. "Text messages read in court nearly lead to a mistrial in Tammy

Moorer case." Myrtle Beach Online, 16 Oct. 2018.

Lohr, David. "Tiffany Daniels Missing: Car Found Abandoned At Florida Beach." Huffington Post, 21 Aug. 2013.

Malloy, Dennis. "It's Been 13 Years Since Mount Laurel Woman Went Missing." Ewing, NJ: New Jersey 101.5 Radio, Townsquare Media, 20 Feb. 2018.

Mims, Bob. "Ex-Tribune employee reported missing." Salt Lake Tribune, 24 Dec. 2009.

Natalie. "The Disappearance of Sky Metalwala." Talk Murder With Me, 26 Jan. 2020.

Renner, James. True Crime Addict: How I Lost Myself in the Mysterious Disappearance of Maura Murray. Thomas Dunne Books/St. Martin's Griffin, 2016.

Rudnick, Natasha. "Suzanne Lyall Missing Since 1998 After Leaving Her Job." CBS News, 27 May 2010.

Salo, Jackie. "The tale of the waitress who messed with the wrong married man." The New York Post, 9 Oct. 2018.

Schwarz, Becca. "10 years later, missing person case remains open." Foothills Gazette, 26 Mar. 2010.

Short, Michelle. "The Unexplained Disappearance of Bryce Laspisa." True Crime Wire, 12 July 2023.

Sullivan, Drew. "Is Brian Shaffer alive?." The Lantern, 12 Apr. 2009.

Sullivan, Michelle. "When Missing Persons Cases Go Cold." Columbus Monthly, Sep. 2014.

Unknown. "The Shocking Disappearance Of Tara Calico And Chilling Polaroids." Owwlogy, 29 May 2022.

Wilson, Charles. "Lauren Spierer case: Men say parents' requests too broad." Lohud, 22 Apr. 2014.

Windnagle, Jordan. "Here's Everything You Need To Know About The Disappearance Of Brandon Lawson." Thought Catalog, 22 Oct. 2020.